Foundations

Foundations

new light on the formation and early years
of the Grand Lodge of England

The Prestonian Lecture

RIC BERMAN

Copyright © 2015 & 2017 Ric Berman
The right of Richard Berman to be identified as the author of this work has been asserted in accordance with the Copyright, Designs and Patents Act, 1988.

The Old Stables Press, Goring Heath, Oxon., RG8 7RT UK.
First published in 2015; reprinted in a revised second edition 2017.

theoldstablespress@gmail.com

All rights reserved. Except for the quotation of short passages for the purposes of criticism and review, no part of this publication may be reproduced, stored in a retrieval system, or transmitted in any form or by any means, without the prior permission of the author.

Images and illustrations are copyright ©UGLE Library & Museum of Freemasonry and used with their kind permission.

British Library Cataloguing in Publication Data
A CIP catalogue record for this book is available from the British Library

Library of Congress Cataloguing-in-Publication Data
Berman, Ric
Foundations: new light on the formation and early years of the Grand Lodge of England/Ric Berman.
p. cm.

ISBN-13: 9780995756816 (The Old Stables Press)
ISBN-10: 0995756813

1. Freemasonry - History – 14th, 15th, 16th, 17th and 18th century. I. Title

For Sue

The sale of this book benefits
The Library & Museum of Freemasonry
60 Great Queen Street, London WC2B 5AZ

Library and Museum Charitable Trust
Registered Charity Number 1058497

Other titles by Ric Berman

*The Foundations of Modern Freemasonry –
The Grand Architects: Political Change and the
Scientific Enlightenment, 1714-1740*

Schism: the Battle that Forged Freemasonry

*Loyalists & Malcontents:
Freemasonry & Revolution in the Deep South*

*Espionage, Diplomacy & the Lodge -
Charles Delafaye and The Secret Department of the
Post Office*

Contents

The Prestonian Lecture · · · · · · · · · · · · · · · · · · · 1
Conclusion · 98
The Library & Museum of Freemasonry · · · · · 100
Friends of the Library & Museum · · · · · · · · · · 112
William Preston and the
Prestonian Lecture · 114
About the Author · 122
The Prestonian Lectures and
Lecturers, 1924-2017 · · · · · · · · · · · · · · · · · · · 128

THE PRESTONIAN LECTURE

Foundations: new light on the formation and early years of the Grand Lodge of England[1]

Ric Berman

John Hamill argued in *The Craft* that there was little evidence to support the theory of a gradual shift in freemasonry from the mediaeval stone masons' guilds to the more gentlemanly 'spiritual' form of Masonic lodge that emerged in the late eighteenth century.[2] But although freemasonry's 'tradition-

---

[1] The contents of this extended version of the 2016 Prestonian Lecture are based on new research material and the author's earlier works: *The Foundations of Modern Freemasonry* (Brighton, 2011) and *Schism: the Battle that Forged Freemasonry* (Brighton, 2013).

[2] John Hamill, *The Craft* (London, 1986), pp. 15-40, quote from pp. 17-8.

al history' may have been queried and rejected by Hamill, no alternative explanation was advanced.[3] The omission was one reason why Hamill's perceptive analysis failed to gain traction and why many freemasons continued (and continue) to cleave to the long-standing if unfounded belief in gradualism, tracing the evolution of the Craft back along a notional thread to 'time immemorial'.

This paper argues that despite those aspects of Masonic ritual that can be dated properly to the medieval period, modern Freemasonry and the Grand Lodge of England emerged in the early decades of the eighteenth century as a consequence of a step-change brought about by new leadership - and not as the inevitable consequence of a continuing trend of measured evolution.

Freemasonry in the early eighteenth century was altered radically over a short period of little more than two decades to mirror the political and philosophical objectives of those who led it. The mind set of those who created and controlled the Grand

---

[3] Jan Snoek, 'Researching Freemasonry. Where Are We?' *CRFF Working Paper Series*, 2 (2008), 1-28.

Lodge of England was determined by many factors but perhaps most significantly by the political, economic and religious insecurity that followed not just successive European wars but also the perceived and real threats posed to the newly installed Hanoverian king - George I - and his Whig government by the Jacobite supporters of the exiled James Stuart – the 'king over the water'.

Although it should be obvious, perhaps even intuitive, that social organisations such as freemasonry are a product of their environment, some historians have considered the relationship to be little more than tangential.[4] The evidence however suggests the opposite: that freemasonry was adapted and moulded – indeed, reinvented - in the second and third decades of the eighteenth century to fit new social and political parameters.

---

[4] *Ibid.*, 20.

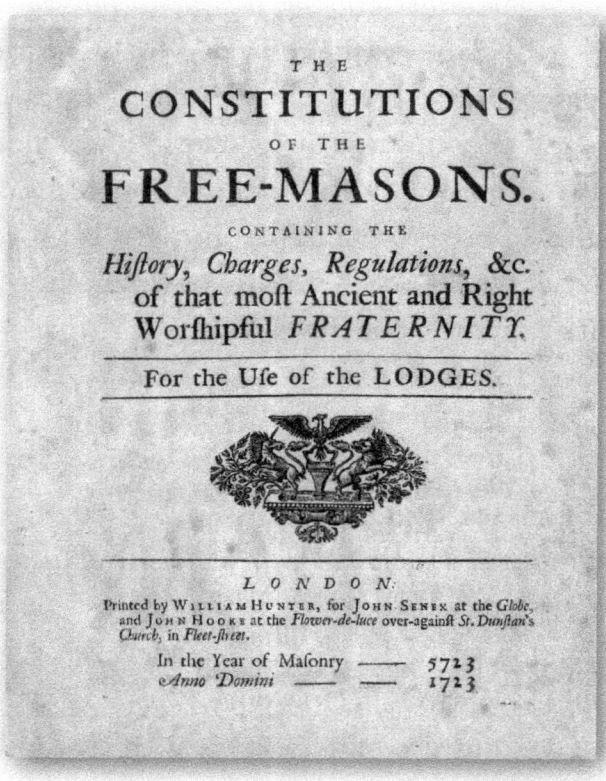

James Anderson's 1723 *Constitutions of the Freemasons*,
Title Page

Among the evidence there is perhaps most obviously the new *Charges* and *Regulations*, the key element of Anderson's 1723 *Constitutions*.[5]

---

[5] James Anderson, *The Constitutions of the Freemasons* (London, 1723).

These were compiled and rewritten by Jean [John] Desaguliers[6] and George Payne[7] to facilitate greater central control over freemasonry and push forward a pro-Hanoverian agenda. Masonic ritual was also altered and lodge meetings flavoured with the new philosophical ideas associated with Newtonian science.[8]

These were not the only changes. Freemasonry continued to evolve and in the second half of the eighteenth century was influenced greatly by the 'Antients' Grand Lodge and by the London Irish.[9] Antients Freemasonry was in part a friendly society

---

[6]   Rev. John Theophilus Desaguliers (1683-1744), Grand Master of Grand Lodge (1719), Deputy Grand Master (1722, 1723 and 1725), a member of the Horn Tavern, Bear & Harrow and the French Lodge.

[7]   George Payne (1685?-1757), Grand Master of Grand Lodge (1718, 1720), Deputy Grand Master (1735), Senior Grand Warden (1724), a member of the Horn Tavern lodge and (in 1749) Master of the King's Arms lodge in the Strand, now the Old King's Arms, No. 28.

[8]   J.T. Desaguliers, *The Newtonian System of the World, the best Model of Government* (Westminster, 1728).

[9]   There is a dispute over whether 'Antients' Freemasonry should be written as 'Antients' or 'Ancients' since both forms of spelling were in use in the eighteenth century. The spelling 'Antients' is used throughout this paper.

and the organisation provided mutual support and a discrete social space for the growing number of aspirational lower middling and working class men who sought to join its membership both in Britain and elsewhere.[10]

But this would be a half-century later. In the early 1720s the Masonic circle at the helm of the Grand Lodge of London & Westminster (later renamed the Grand Lodge of England) intentionally positioned it as a vehicle to reconfigure English Freemasonry.

The construct that emerged was materially different from that which had gone before and became within two decades the most prominent of Britain's many fraternal societies with a membership that probably exceeded 4,000.[11] And the new freemasonry was not limited to London. Within a few years it could boast a uniquely large provincial network and a presence overseas where its growth was facilitated by immigration, military expansion and

---

[10] Berman, *Schism*.
[11] Peter Clark, *British Clubs and Societies 1580-1800* (Oxford, 2000).

political influence, alongside British and colonial trade.[12]

In addition to its pro-Hanoverian characteristics and Whig political affiliation, English Freemasonry's leadership associated the organisation with science and the Enlightenment - with a world that could be measured and explained. They also connected it to antiquarianism and the growing desire in the eighteenth century to understand and explore the past.

Equally if not more appealing to its members and potential members was freemasonry's strong association with and support from celebrated members of the aristocracy, its seeming exclusivity, and its well-publicised and clubbable fraternal drinking and dining.

A contemporary rhyme described this aspect of the Craft succinctly:

---

[12] Jessica Harland-Jacobs, *Builders of Empire: Freemasonry and British Imperialism, 1717-1927* (Chapel Hill, 2007), pp. 1-20.

> *We make for Five guineas, the price is but small,*
> *And then Lords and Dukes, you your Brothers may call,*
> *Have gloves, a White Apron, get drunk and that's all.* [13]

English Freemasonry in the 1720s and 1730s captured the contemporary zeitgeist. And its success was such that copies emerged rapidly elsewhere. Lodges and later grand lodges were established not only across the home nations but also in many countries within Europe, including France, the Netherlands, Sweden, Austria, Germany and Russia, as well as in Italy, Portugal and Spain.

Nevertheless, in parts of continental Europe, freemasonry's following among the aristocracy, the military, intellectuals and politicians gave rise to concern and opposition, especially among the senior ranks of the Catholic Church who believed freemasonry to be a threat to their authority.

---

[13] A Gentleman, *Love's last shift: or, the mason disappointed* … (London, *c.*1720).

A papal bull from Pope Clement XII denouncing freemasonry was issued on 28 April 1738. Although the bull acknowledged that freemasonry was interdenominational, composed of 'men of any religion or sect, satisfied with the appearance of natural probity, [and] joined together, according to their laws and the statutes laid down for them, by a strict and unbreakable bond',[14] private discussion in societies where debate was otherwise circumscribed was not tolerated easily. Moreover and in addition to any perceived threat to national security, 'if they were not doing evil they would not have so great a hatred of the light'.[15]

Freemasonry was perceived by Pope Clement as posing an existential threat to 'the peace of the temporal state' and to Catholic teaching by challenging the authority of the church. Over time it would be opposed by the threat of excommunication, and in Spain, Italy and elsewhere by periodic waves of prohibition and restriction.

---

[14] *In Eminenti*, Papal Bull of Pope Clement XII, 28 April 1738.
[15] *Ibid.* Cf. also Jürgen Habermas, transl. Thomas Burger, *The Structural Transformation of the Public Sphere: An Inquiry into a Category of Bourgeois Society* (Cambridge, 1989).

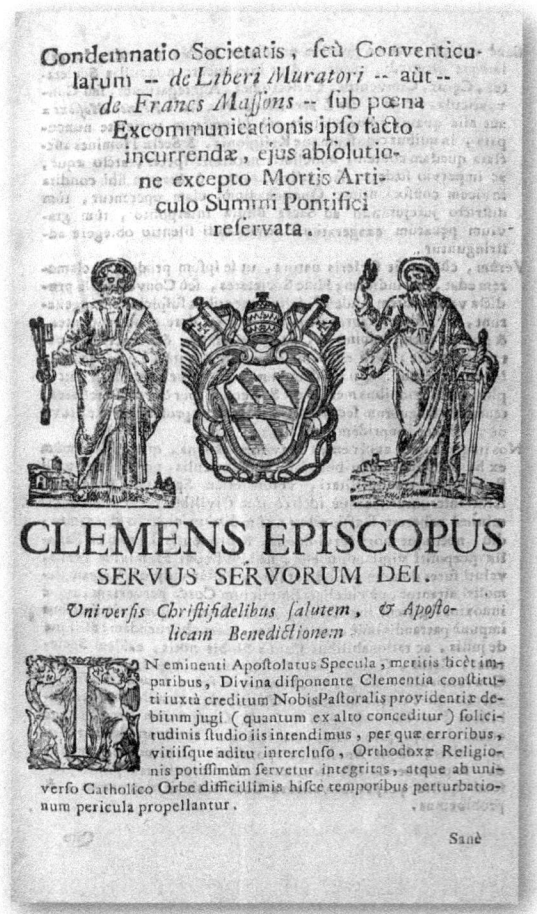

Pope Clement XII's *In Eminenti Apostolatus Specula*

But despite this opposition, freemasonry grew in popularity to the extent that the Masonic lodge came to be positioned close to the heart of eighteenth-century sociability. This was not only the case across

Foundations

Europe but also in America and elsewhere in Britain's growing Empire.¹⁶

The development was momentous and to understand its significance and to gain a sense of perspective it is necessary to go back three centuries before the creation of the Grand Lodge of London & Westminster to mediaeval England.

Some commentators have argued that the pursuit of a single point of origin for English Freemasonry should be regarded as unproductive – as a dead end.¹⁷ Nonetheless, if one were to search for such a point it would be hard to ignore the tectonic shift in the economic and social fabric that accompanied and followed the Black Death in 1348.

---

¹⁶ Pierre-Yves Beaurepaire, 'The Universal Republic of the Freemasons and the Culture of Mobility in the Enlightenment', *French Historical Studies*, 29.3 (2006), 407-31.

¹⁷ Andrew Prescott, 'The Old Charges Revisited', *Transactions of the Lodge of Research, No. 2429*, Leicester (2006).

The soaring mortality brought about by the outbreak of what was a plague pandemic led to widespread shortages and market dislocations which triggered a sharp rise in the cost of labour.[18] The government reacted by passing anti-labour legislation in an attempt to suppress wage rates.[19] Approved in 1349, Edward III's *Ordinance of Labourers* was designed to cut labourers' pay to the levels that had applied in 1346 before the Black Death. The *Statute of Labourers* enacted in 1351 reinforced the regulations by imposing piecework and daily wage rates for specific occupations. And other laws followed.

The obligation to enforce this legislation was incorporated by statute into the duties of the magistracy and by the end of the fourteenth century local

---

[18] David Loschky and Ben D. Childers, 'Early English Mortality', *Journal of Interdisciplinary History*, 24.1 (1993), 85-97; Faye Marie Getz, 'Black Death and the Silver Lining' *Journal of the History of Biology*, 24.2 (1991), 265-89.

[19] L.R. Poos, 'The Social Context of Statute of Labourers Enforcement', *Law and History Review*, 1.1 (1983), 27-52; and Chris Given-Wilson, 'The Problem of Labour in the Context of the English Government, *c.* 1350-1450', in Bothwell, Goldberg and Ormrod (eds.), *The Problem of Labour in Fourteenth-Century England* (York, 2000), pp. 85-100.

justices of the peace had been empowered to determine at their discretion the deemed 'reasonable' maximum wage rates for their districts. Other laws restricted labour mobility and skewed the terms of contracts in favour of employers.[20]

The landowner-dominated parliament that enacted this anti-worker legislation had a vested interest in ensuring that inexpensive labour was available for their estates. Such landowners, the gentry and others from their circles also served as local magistrates with responsibility for enforcing the law. The conflict between the landed interest and agricultural and artisanal labour was clear. And it persisted in the wake of further outbreaks of plague throughout the latter half of the century. It resulted in one of the best known examples of resistance to parliamentary diktat: the Peasants' Revolt of 1381, a

---

[20] Cf., Chris Given-Wilson, 'Service, Serfdom and English Labour Legislation, 1350-1500' in Anne Curry and Elizabeth Matthew (eds.), *Concepts and Patterns of Service in the later Middle Ages* (Woodbridge, 2000), pp. 21-37.

movement catalysed by parliament's imposition of higher taxes.[21]

But despite laws to the contrary, the government was unable to legislate away the economic reality of demand and supply. Faced with a labour shortage, the nominal cash wages of skilled building workers in southern England rose by two-thirds over the second half of the fourteenth century, from 3*d* per day in the mid-1340s to 5*d* per day in the 1390s. During the same period the pay rate of unskilled labourers doubled from around 1½*d* to 3*d* per day.[22] Indeed, adjusted for inflation, the real wages of artisans rose

---

[21] W.M. Ormrod, 'The Peasants' Revolt and the Government of England', *Journal of British Studies*, 29.1 (1990), 1-30. Also, R.S. Gottfried, 'Population, Plague, and the Sweating Sickness: Demographic Movements in Late Fifteenth-Century England', *Journal of British Studies*, 17.1 (1977), 12-37; Mark Bailey, 'Demographic Decline in Late Medieval England: Some Thoughts', *Economic History Review*, n.s. 49.1 (1996), 1-19.

[22] Henry Phelps-Brown and Sheila V. Hopkins, *A Perspective of Wages and Prices* (London, 1981), pp. 3-61. Cf. also, Simon A.C. Penn and Christopher Dyer, 'Wages and Earnings in Late Medieval England: Evidence from the Enforcement of the Labour Laws', *Economic History Review*, n.s. 43.3 (1990), 356-76.

by around 45% and those of unskilled workers by some 60%.

Nonetheless, in the following century the position altered dramatically. Knoop and Jones in *The Mediaeval Mason*[23] draw a graphic portrait of this unfolding as real wage increases reversed and then declined across much of England during the fifteenth, sixteenth and seventeenth centuries as prices increased more than six-fold and pay rates failed to maintain parity.

The principal trigger for what became sustained price inflation was the unprecedented expansion of money supply linked to the flow of New World bullion to Europe, alongside large-scale silver mining in central Europe[24] and the debasement of English coinage by successive monarchs.[25]

---

[23] Douglas Knoop and G.P Jones, *The Mediaeval Mason* (Manchester, 1933), p. 206.

[24] John Munro, 'The Monetary Origins of the 'Price Revolution': South German Silver Mining, Merchant-Banking, and Venetian Commerce, 1470-1540', *University of Toronto, Dept. of Economics Working Paper*, 8 June 1999, rev. 21 March 2003.

[25] G. Davies, *A History of Money from Ancient Times to the Present Day* (Cardiff, 1996), revised edn., pp. 187, 197-206.

But despite falling real wages, England's labour markets continued to be characterised by hostile legislation and local pay negotiations threatened by judicial sanction.

The subsequent decline in earnings for stone masons and other workers – both skilled and manual – set the context for the transformation of what previously had been predominantly religious guilds into operative guilds. It also saw the advent of pay rates established through local collective bargaining. Both were visible parts of a process through which craftsmen began to combine for their mutual economic benefit and protection.

The changes were reflected clearly in the scope and content of the *Old Charges*, the first written evidence of early English Freemasonry.[26]

The *Cooke* and *Regius* manuscripts mention pay specifically and each argues hard that employers should pay wages that accommodate inflation:

---

[26] Berman, *The Foundations of Modern Freemasonry*, Appendix Two.

pay thy felows after the coste as vytaylys goth thenne ... and pay them trwly, apon thy fay, what that they deserve.[27]

It was from this period that artisans, including stone masons, carpenters and other trades, established more formally what were effectively 'closed shops' to create and sustain local monopolies in order to control labour supply and influence its price and profitability.[28] Local guilds imposed restrictive employment practices using the justification of better training and quality control, as well as contract enforcement, alongside other arguments. Membership – in effect, the supply of labour - was controlled by the guilds, who limited the number of apprenticeships and established a minimum period for training.

In broad terms, the guilds' actions were designed to influence and support the price of their members' labour, and to protect what they regarded as their

---

[27] The *Halliwell* or *Regius* MS. The manuscript is dated to the early fifteenth century.
[28] Cf., for example, Ernest L. Sabine, 'Butchering in Medieval London', *Speculum*, 8.3 (1933), 335-53.

proprietary skills from untrained 'cowans' – outsiders who had not served a regular apprenticeship.[29]

Although the guilds also provided a rudimentary framework for mutual financial assistance and low level education, this was secondary to their principal function of influencing wage rates, protecting their members' privileges and, most importantly, maintaining or protecting real earnings.[30] The process has been termed a 'syndicalist phase' and it is hard not to concur.[31]

Having been admitted to a stone masons' guild, a new member would progress through three stages from initiation, that is, acceptance into the guild as an apprentice, through to the intermediate position of

---

[29] Cf. Avner Greif, Paul Milgrom, Barry R. Weingast, 'Coordination, Commitment, and Enforcement: The Case of the Merchant Guild', *Journal of Political Economy*, 102.4 (1994), 745-66, for a review of the origins of and justification for medieval merchant guilds.

[30] Cf. Gervase Rosser, 'Crafts, Guilds and the Negotiation of Work in the Medieval Town', *Past & Present*, 154 (1997), 3-31, for an insight into the reconfiguration of craft guild structures.

[31] Andrew Prescott, 'A History of British Freemasonry 1425-2000', *CRFF Working Paper Series 1*, (2008).

'craftsman' or 'journeyman', and finally to the completion of the apprenticeship when a journeyman would be accorded the status of a master mason.

Upon initiation and at each stage of the progression from apprentice to fellowcraft, and fellowcraft to master mason, the candidate would swear an oath to keep secret the guild's operational methodology. In return he would be entrusted with the working secrets appropriate to each new rank and with a password, sign and token. The training would last for at least seven years; the usual age at entry was fourteen and the minimum age to be raised to the status of a master mason was twenty-one, the legal age of maturity.

The rate at which a candidate progressed was a function of tradition, skill and economic conditions. There was little point in allowing an apprentice to advance if insufficient work was available; conversely, financial advantages accrued to master masons through their exploitation of apprentices - in practice indentured labour - during periods of high demand.

Stone masons' skills were fundamental to the construction of the abbeys, cathedrals, churches, mansions, town halls and city walls that commanded the religious and secular heights of medieval society. As a result - and unlike many other craftsmen and the majority of agricultural labourers - skilled stone masons had qualified flexibility to travel to work on different construction sites.[32]

It has been argued that this relative autonomy is the explanation of the term 'freemason'. There are however alternative and rather more robust explanations. One is that the word derives from a shortened form of 'Freestone Mason', referring to a skilled mason qualified to work with freestone: the best form of stone, capable of being worked without shattering. Since freestone was one of the more expensive types of stone, a mason would usually be fully trained before being permitted to work it. Such skilled masons

---

[32] J.A. Raftis, *Peasant Economic Development within the English Manorial System*, (Montreal, 1996), provides an analysis of early agrarian capitalism, labour segmentation and mobility. It follows his pioneering work, *Tenure and Mobility* (Toronto, 1964).

were thus called 'free masons' in order to distinguish them from 'rough' or ordinary masons.[33]

Knoop and Jones reached a similar conclusion, albeit via a different route, arguing perhaps more probably that 'free' had been derived linguistically from 'noble' or 'superior' and that the term was used to imply a skilled worker able to command a premium rate of pay over and above a rough or less expert mason.[34]

Contemporary records hold numerous examples of the term being used in this way. One example is from a petition supporting a Richard Hardwick of Shepton Mallet who had been indicted for working as a 'free mason' when qualified only as a 'rough mason'.[35]

Over the course of the sixteenth and seventeenth centuries the guilds' social and financial influence increased steadily as they became integrated into and embedded within local civic political structures,

---

[33] Jan Snoek, *Initiating Women into Freemasonry* (Leiden, 2012), p. 1.
[34] Knoop and Jones, *The Mediaeval Mason*, pp. 86-9.
[35] Somerset Archive and Record Service: Rough General: Order Books Q/SOr *1613-1887*.

especially in London and England's larger provincial cities, including Chester and York.

In addition to their local and regional political influence, which included nominating members to the city council, a range of social and financial connections tied the guilds to the municipal authorities and *vice versa*.[36] At the same time guild membership shifted, becoming increasingly dominated by master builders and business owners.[37]

Such men had a similar social standing to other civic burghers and freemen and comparable economic interests. Heather Swanson,[38] commenting on and extending Maurice Dobb's (Marxist) analysis,[39] has argued that local merchant and artisan oligarchies controlled provincial towns and cities and manipulated the guild system to advance their own self-interested

---

[36] P.M. Tillott (ed.), *A History of the County of York* (London, 1961), pp. 91-7, 166-73 & 173-86.

[37] Knoop and Jones, *The Mediaeval Mason*, pp. 223-33.

[38] Heather Swanson, 'The Illusion of Economic Structure: Craft Guilds in Late Mediaeval English Towns', *Past & Present*, 121 (1988), 29-48, esp. 30-1.

[39] Maurice Dobb, *Studies in the Development of Capitalism* (London, 1946), p. 97.

political and financial purposes. And as Dobb noted, the prevailing condition of relatively inefficient and parochial markets facilitated such exploitation:

> *monopoly was of the essence of economic life in this epoch ... since the municipal authority had the right to make regulations as to who should trade and when they should trade; it possessed a considerable power of turning the balance of trade in [its own] favour.*[40]

Self-interest also encouraged guilds to admit local dignitaries to their ranks. The advantages were tangible since the local magistrates' authority still extended to setting wage rates based on local market conditions; indeed, the practice had been reaffirmed in the sixteenth-century *Statute of Artificers*.[41] Moreover, local politicians - aldermen, sheriffs and mayors - were responsible for commissioning civic building works and granting guild charters, and the higher fees paid by non-working members effectively provided a subsidy to the lodge.

---

[40] *Ibid.*, pp. 89-90.
[41] Woodward, 'The Background to the Statute of Artificers: The genesis of Labour Policy, 1558-63', *Economic History Review*, n.s. 33.1 (1980), 32-44.

This 'functionalist' interpretation has been put forward not only by Marxist historians but also by Masonic historians. Referring to 'a very old manuscript', William Preston noted at the end of the eighteenth century that

> *when the Master and Wardens met in a lodge, if need be, the sheriff of the county, or the mayor of the city, or alderman of the town, in which the congregation is held, should be made fellow and sociate to the Master, in help of him against rebels.*[42]

In short, the mutual economic advantages were obvious. In return for granting the guilds the privilege of operating local or regional monopolies, the municipalities received fees, taxes and a share in the fines levied by the guilds. And by admitting non-operative members, the guilds developed a close relationship with their clients and prospective clients, and enhanced their influence over the availability and thus the price of labour. Moreover, with both groups increasingly overlapping, it can be argued – probably correctly – that members of the local

---

[42] William Preston, *Illustrations of Masonry* (London, 1796), p. 184.

oligarchy eventually dominated both sides of the negotiating table.[43]

This status quo endured until the second half of the seventeenth century when changes to working practices, combined with disquiet at the guilds' conservatism and what came to be seen as their unenlightened opposition to innovation and free trade, led them to be criticised as a brake on commercial progress, a perspective that led to a reduction in their role and authority.[44]

Throughout the period up to the end of the seventeenth century and notwithstanding changes to form and function, the masons' guilds - in common with other guilds - retained elements of their past ritual, including passwords, codes of conduct and traditional histories - the *Old Charges*.

---

[43] With regard to York, cf., R.B. Dobson, 'Admissions to the Freedom of the City of York in the Later Middle Ages', *Economic History Review*, n.s. 26.1 (1973), 1-22, and Swanson, 'The Illusion of Economic Structure', 46-8.

[44] Cf. Sheilagh Ogilvie, 'Guilds, Efficiency, and Social Capital: Evidence from German Proto-Industry', *Economic History Review*, n.s. 57.2 (2004), 286-333, for a complementary perspective on the German guilds.

The *Old Charges* had not been designed and written as an accurate historical record but rather to give freemasonry legitimacy in a tradition-based society by dating the Craft's origins to the distant past. The *Cooke* MS, for example, asserted that freemasonry was introduced 'seven generations' after Adam:

> *before Noah's flood, there was a man that was named Lamech ... he begat two sons ... [and] the elder son, Jabal, was the first man that ever found geometry and Masonry.*[45]

And where the *Regius* and other early manuscripts dated the arrival of freemasonry in England to King Athelstan, an Anglo-Saxon king reigning in the early tenth century, *Cooke* pushed the date back even further to the third century and St Alban,[46] one of the earliest English Christian martyrs, noting that 'Saint Alban loved well masons, and he gave them first their charges and manners first in England'.[47]

---

[45] *Cooke* MS, lines 160-80.
[46] St Alban, a Christian convert, was martyred by the Romans at Verulamium (now St Albans). The precise date of death is not known.
[47] *Cooke* MS, lines 605-9.

Perhaps more importantly, *Cooke* stated that the level of (contemporary) wage rates had been approved by King Athelstan, who had also given his imprimatur to Masonic guilds and lodge assemblies:

> *and he loved well masonry and masons. And he became a mason himself, and he gave them charges and names as it is now used in England, and in other countries. And he ordained that they should have reasonable pay and purchased a free patent of the king that they should make [an] assembly when they saw a reasonable time.*[48]

It was no coincidence that the York manuscripts written in the mid-sixteenth century similarly echoed contemporary labour discontent.[49] Nor that the wages demanded by the striking craftsmen in 1552 were virtually identical to those set out in contemporary Masonic histories that referred to the rates of pay applicable centuries earlier during the time of St Alban - '2*s* 6*d* a week for work and 3*d* a day for food'.[50]

---

[48] *Ibid.*, lines 625-37.
[49] Prescott, 'The Old Charges Revisited'.
[50] *Ibid.*

The evidence is compelling in that each version of the *Old Charges* – whether written in the fifteenth, sixteenth or seventeenth century – closely reflected the contemporary context. References to St Athelstan and St Alban simply provided a framework in which technically illegal wage negotiation and collective bargaining could be defended on moral grounds and through historical precedent. And allowed higher wage rates to be justified on the same basis.

Nonetheless, during the seventeenth century the *Charges* and *Regulations* are likely to have become less important for their substance than their form, as lodge meetings morphed to mirror the altered composition and status of their more gentrified members with gatherings that were increasingly dominated by social rather than operative considerations.

The admission of gentlemen to the lodge has often been advanced as evidence of the beginning of 'spiritual' – or 'speculative' - freemasonry. But although gentleman freemasons such as Elias Ashmole and other antiquaries may indeed have been motivated in part by a desire to experience esoteric lodge traditions, many, probably most, had different motives.

A minority of gentlemen members may have acted as lodge benefactors, attending only rarely and in a parallel capacity to a patron of a religious order. But for most gentlemen, local business and political networking, accompanied by fraternal socialising - dining and drinking - would have been the main rationale for joining the lodge.

Gervase Rosser commented that 'feasting and drinking were in the Middle Ages regarded as [the] defining activities of the guilds':[51] 'if it were not for the feasting, few or none would come'.[52] Rosser also notes the ritualistic and charitable aspects of the annual feast and its function in the fifteenth and sixteenth centuries as a means whereby 'links of solidarity and patronage could be forged'.[53]

There is little reason to believe that the position was fundamentally different in the seventeenth century and that gentlemen entered the lodge for reasons that had little to do with spirituality other than

---

[51] Gervase Rosser, 'Going to the Fraternity Feast: Commensality and Social Relations in Late Medieval England', *Journal of British Studies*, 33.4 (1994), 430-46.
[52] *Ibid.*, 431.
[53] *Ibid.*, esp. 433-438, quote from 438.

in the sense that almost every act in mediaeval and later society through to the late seventeenth century had a 'spiritual' component.

In summary, guilds that admitted affluent members of the gentry and other 'city fathers' benefitted from the subsidy that their fees represented and from their business and political connections.[54] Indeed, several lodges, including those in Warrington, Chester and York, evolved to the point where their members comprised a majority of non-operative masons. The surviving membership records suggest that over time such non-working members perpetuated their influence through invitations to friends and successive generations of family to the extent that their lodges became predominantly fraternal organisations - clubs - where

---

[54] Cf. Jacob, *Living the Enlightenment* (Oxford, 1991), pp. 38-40. The example of a Dundee operative Masonic guild which provided non-Masons or 'strangers' with the benefit of 'freedom' of the guild upon payment of £10, is a clear (albeit Scottish) instance of the principle of admitting non-Masons to alleviate financial problems.

dining and networking took precedence over other activities.⁵⁵

The point was recognised by Neville Barker Cryer. When reflecting on the status of members of the Chester Masonic lodge in the seventeenth century⁵⁶ he noted that by the 1660s the lodge was 'made up largely of the city fathers'.⁵⁷ Indeed, Lewis and Thacker's *History of the County of Chester* makes a similar point.⁵⁸

Barker Cryer's commentary on York Freemasonry in 1705 also supports the argument. The city's lodge membership included many of its first families and freemasonry had the 'support and patronage of significant Yorkshire gentry'. In Barker Cryer's words,

---

⁵⁵ R.F. Gould, *The History of Freemasonry: Its Antiquities, Symbols, Constitutions, Customs, Etc.* (Edinburgh, 1900), vol. 2, pp. 264-6, provides such an analysis of the 1646 lodge meeting at Warrington. (Originally published London, 1885.)
⁵⁶ Neville Barker Cryer, 'The Restoration Lodge of Chester', November Conference of the Cornerstone Society, 2002.
⁵⁷ Neville Barker Cryer, *York Mysteries Revealed* (York, 2006), p. 222.
⁵⁸ C.P. Lewis and A.T. Thacker, *A History of the County of Chester: The City of Chester* (2003), vol. 5, part 1, pp. 102-9.

by the beginning of the eighteenth century, York's Freemasonry had carved out a 'notable niche for itself socially'.[59]

Engraving of Elias Ashmole by William Faithorne (*c*.1620-1691) originally published in 1656

The same analysis is applicable to Staffordshire Freemasonry, reports of which were penned by Elias

---

[59] Barker Cryer, *York Mysteries Revealed*, p. 222.

Ashmole,[60] John Aubrey[61] and Robert Plot,[62] each of whom underscored the presence of gentlemen and non-operative freemasons in the lodge. Although their work has also been put forward as evidence of a move towards spiritual freemasonry in the seventeenth century, the presence of gentlemen within a lodge and their description as 'freemasons' as opposed to 'masons' neither indicates nor suggests that English Freemasonry was in transition. It proves only that gentlemen were present within the lodge. Indeed, that this had been the position for more than a century is not contentious.

It is probable that the most commonly cited (albeit faux) demonstration of the existence of 'speculative' freemasonry in the seventeenth century concerns Elias Ashmole, the antiquary and founder of the University of Oxford's Ashmolean museum.[63] His *Memoirs* document two Masonic events: his initiation in Warrington on 16 October 1646, and his

---

[60] Elias Ashmole, *Memoirs of the life of that learned antiquary, Elias Ashmole, Esq; drawn up by himself by way of diary* (London, 1717).
[61] John Aubrey, *The Natural History of Wiltshire* (Oxford, 1691).
[62] Robert Plot, *The Natural history of Staffordshire* (Oxford, 1686).
[63] Elias Ashmole (1617-1692).

attendance at a lodge at the Company of Masons' Hall in London on 11 March 1682.

Ashmole's diary entries have been interpreted as offering confirmation that in the mid-seventeenth century gentlemen who in William Stukeley's words were 'interested in the mysteries of the Ancients'[64] became members of working stone masons lodges and were thus part of a transitioning to speculative freemasonry. Gould, for example, stated that 'it is obvious that symbolical masonry must have existed in Lancashire for some time before the admission of Ashmole and Mainwaring'.[65]

This is more an assertion than an argument and there is an alternative analysis that suggests that Ashmole's interest in freemasonry was more probably

---

[64] William Stukeley, (W.C. Lukis (ed.)), *Family Memoirs of William Stukeley* (London, 1883), vol. 1, p. 51.
[65] R.F. Gould, *The Concise History of Freemasonry* (London, 1951), revised edn., p. 113.

a function of social networking than derived from his interest in antiquarianism and alchemy.[66]

In his diary entry dated 16 October 1646, Ashmole recorded that he 'was made a Freemason at Warrington in Lancashire with Col. Henry Mainwaring of Kerthingham in Cheshire'. He also gave the names of others then in the lodge: 'Mr Richard Penkett Warden, Mr James Collier, Mr Richard Sankey, Henry Littler, John Ellam, Ricard Ellam, and Hugh Brewer'.[67]

Another entry dated 10 March 1682 stated that 'about 5 p.m. I [Ashmole] received a Summons to appear at a lodge to be held the next day at Masons' Hall in London';[68] and the entry for the following day, 11 March, set out the events thereafter:

---

[66] M. Jacob, *The Radical Enlightenment*, p. 107, fn. 12. Jacob cites R.D. Gray, *Goethe, the Alchemist* (Cambridge, 1952), pp. 49, 177 and *passim*, for evidence of a relationship between eighteenth-century Masonic symbolism and the alchemical tradition.
[67] Ashmole, *Memoirs*, pp. 15-6.
[68] *Ibid.*, p. 66.

> *Accordingly I went, and about Noon were admitted into the Fellowship of Freemasons,*[69] *Sir William Wilson, Knight, Capt. Richard Borthwick, Mr William Woodman, Mr William Grey, Mr Samuel Taylour, and Mr William Wise. I was the Senior Fellow among them (it being 35 Years since I was admitted) ... We all dined at the Half-Moon-Tavern in Cheapside, at a Noble Dinner prepared at the Charge of the new accepted Masons.*[70]

Ashmole's *Memoirs* comprise brief notes probably for an unwritten autobiography. The entry for 16 October 1646 is significant only because it is the first contemporary record of the admittance of a non-operative freemason in England (although those recorded as present by Ashmole would obviously have already been admitted as masons).

---

[69] *Ibid.* In the posthumous publication of the *Memoirs* in 1717, the word 'by' appears after 'Fellowship of Freemasons'. The word is not present in Ashmole's original manuscript and has also been omitted above. The omission may be important in that 'by' could signify that Sir William Wilson was already a freemason. I am grateful to Prof. Aubrey Newman for this observation.

[70] *Ibid.*, pp. 66-7.

The details of Ashmole's initiation are non-existent but it is clear that the lodge members mentioned by him were of a similar social standing. Rylands set out the evidence in the *Masonic Magazine* in the 1880s and concluded at that time that few or none of those attending the lodge were working stone masons.[71] His analysis is supported by Tobias Churton who wrote a century later that the lodge was 'largely made up of landed gentry from Cheshire and from that county's border with south Lancashire'.[72] Churton also pointed to the connection between gentleman landowners and fraternalism' and put forward a conjecture that the dominant aspect of lodge membership was social. This interpretation is supported by Peter Kebbell's

---

[71] *The Masonic Magazine: A Monthly Digest of Freemasonry in All Its Branches*. The magazine was published in London by George Kenning. The relevant article by W.H. Rylands, 'Freemasonry in Seventeenth Century Warrington', appeared in the December 1881 issue. Cf. George M. Martin, *British Masonic Miscellany, Part 2* (Whitefish, 2003), p. 25. Also cf., for example, Gould, *The Concise History of Freemasonry* (London, 1951), revised edn., pp. 112-3. Rylands' collection of Masonic manuscripts was donated to the Bodleian: MSS Rylands, b. 1-11, c. 1-30, c. 32-8, c. 40-69, d. 1-57, e. 1-54, f. 1-9.

[72] T. Churton, *Freemasonry – The Reality*, pp. 172-9, 273

observation that Ashmole was personally connected to Henry Mainwaring: Peter Mainwaring, a relative, was Ashmole's father-in-law.[73]

Ashmole's attendance at a lodge at the London Masons' Company in 1682 and his note describing that event suggests that the invitation was to a meeting of the 'Acception', an exclusive inner lodge within the larger setting of the Masons' Company.

> *Sir William Wilson, Knight, Capt. Richard Borthwick, Mr William Woodman, Mr William Grey, Mr Samuel Taylour, and Mr William Wise ...*
>
> *Present beside myself ... [were] Mr Thomas Wise, Master of the Masons Company this present Year; Mr Thomas Shorthose, Mr Thomas Shadbolt, - Waindsfford, Esq.; Mr Nicholas Young, Mr John Shorthose, Mr William Hamon, Mr John Thompson, and Mr William Stanton.*

---

[73] Peter Kebbell, *The Changing Face of Freemasonry, 1640-1740* (University of Bristol, unpublished PhD Thesis, 2009), pp. 23-5.

Eight of the nine named in the second paragraph were already members of the Masons' Company as were Sir William Wilson[74] and William Woodman.[75] Three of the (presumed) initiates, William Grey, Samuel Taylour and William Wise, the son of the Master of the Company, were also members.[76]

The composition of the initiates, members and guests implies that the Acception was not a 'speculative' lodge open to non-operative members such as Ashmole, but rather an inner circle of élite masons who could also be regarded as gentlemen.

Thomas Wise, the Master of the Masons' Company, was an eminent stonemason who had worked with Sir Christopher Wren on the

---

[74] Sir William Wilson (1641-1710).

[75] Cf., Gould, *The Concise History of Freemasonry*, pp. 115-8.

[76] It is clear that some of those present were initiates since *We all dined at the Half-Moon-Tavern ...* <u>*at the Charge of the new accepted Masons*</u>. If 'by' is included, then the text could read ... *and about Noon were admitted into the Fellowship of Freemasons [by] Sir William Wilson, Knight, [the initiates:] Capt. Richard Borthwick, Mr William Woodman, Mr William Grey, Mr Samuel Taylour, and Mr William Wise.*

construction of Chelsea Hospital.[77] He was supported at the meeting by his Wardens, John Shorthose and William Stanton, indicating that the meeting had formal sanction. Indeed, Prescott has commented that members of the Masons' Company admitted to the Acception were recorded publicly on panels in the Company's livery hall and that the Acception paraded under its own banner.[78]

It is possible that Sir William Wilson's presence in or admission to the inner circle of the Acception was the catalyst for Ashmole's attendance. Wilson was a stonemason of standing. He had married into the Staffordshire gentry and been knighted in 1681, probably through the influence of Jane Pudsey, his future wife.[79] They had met when Wilson had been commissioned to sculpt a memorial to her late husband and Pudsey may have been unwilling to marry

---

[77] 'Entry for 20 March, 1684', *Money Book*, vol. IV, pp. 355-6, in William A Shaw (ed.), *Calendar of Treasury Books* (London, 1916), vol. 7, p. 1077.
[78] Prescott, 'The Old Charges Revisited'.
[79] George T. Noszlopy and Fiona Waterhouse, *Public Sculpture of Staffordshire and the Black Country* (Liverpool, 2005), illustrated edn., p. 273.

a social inferior; a knighthood provided the required social elevation.

Wilson worked mainly in the Midlands, especially Lichfield and Sutton Coldfield, and in 1669 had sculpted the statue of Charles II erected at Lichfield Cathedral.[80]

Ashmole was also connected to Lichfield. He had been born in the city, studied there as a cathedral chorister and was one of the cathedral's chief benefactors. He had also stood for election as Lichfield's parliamentary candidate, albeit unsuccessfully.[81]

Ashmole's summons to the Acception suggests that his freemasonry was known to members of the Staffordshire gentry, including Wilson. Moreover, beyond this connection, Ashmole's social position and wealth would have helped to secure an invitation. Ashmole's royalist politics had been rewarded after the Restoration and in 1660 he had been appointed Comptroller of the Excise and in 1668 Accountant General. Both positions

---

[80] *Ibid.*, pp. xxv, 198-9, 235-6, 270, 277, 292-3.
[81] Michael Hunter, 'Elias Ashmole (1617–1692)', *Oxford Dictionary of National Biography*, hereafter '*ODNB*'.

were well-remunerated and offered scope for patronage. Ashmole's own patron, James Pagitt, a relation through his mother, was Baron of the Exchequer.[82]

And Ashmole held other sinecures, not least Windsor Herald at the College of Arms, a position he retained from 1660 until his resignation in 1675.[83] Moreover, alongside Sir Robert Moray, another (Scottish) freemason,[84] he had status as one of the

---

[82] Ashmole had previously held office as Commissioner for the Excise at Lichfield (1644) and Commissioner at Worcester (1644-1646).

[83] 'An account by Elias Ashmole, then Windsor Herald, of the Feast of the Exaltation of the Cross, and a transcription of the Greek and Latin inscription on a medal struck by the Emperor Heraclius': Lambeth Palace Library: MS 929, *1611-1723*, 43, 2 ff.

[84] Sir Robert Moray had been initiated into freemasonry when serving with the Scottish forces besieging Newcastle-upon-Tyne. His admittance into St Mary's Chapel Lodge of Edinburgh was recorded on 20 May 1641. Cf. David Allan, 'Sir Robert Moray (1608/9?–1673)', *ODNB*.

Foundations

founding Fellows of the Royal Society of London.[85] Last but by no means least, Ashmole was the chief benefactor and founder of Oxford's Ashmolean, established in 1682, perhaps not coincidentally the year he was invited to attend the Accption.

Rather than gathering for purely 'speculative' or 'spiritual' purposes, the Acception's records indicate that fraternal dining was a central element of each meeting. A reference to an earlier meeting of the Acception in 1638 recorded in the Renter Warden's Accounts of the Company of Masons notes that five masons were 'taken into the Accepcon [sic]', each paying a fee of ten shillings:[86]

> *Pd wch the accompt layd out wch was more than he received of them wch were taken into the Accepcon whereof Xs is to be paid by Mr*

---

[85] Cf. C.H. Josten (ed.), *Elias Ashmole (1617–1692): His Autobiographical and Historical Notes* (Oxford, 1966). The Royal Society was formed in 1660 and granted a royal charter on 15 July 1662; a second royal charter extending its rights was granted by Charles II on 22 April 1663.

[86] Matthew Scanlan, 'Nicholas Stone and the Mystery of the Acception', *Freemasonry Today*, 12 (2002); and 'The Mystery of the Acception, 1630-1723: A Fatal Flaw', *Heredom*, 11 (2003).

Nicholas Stone, Mr Edmund Kinsman, Mr John Smith, Mr William Millis, Mr John Colles.[87]

The fee provides confirmation that membership was not open to the ordinary mason: 10*s* was equivalent to a month's wages at a time when an average stonemason might earn some 4*d* - 6*d* per day.[88]

Nicholas Stone is an important figure in the extract.[89] He was appointed Master Mason at Windsor Castle in 1626 and the King's Master Mason in 1632, in which year he was elected Master of the Company of Masons. He was re-elected the following year and had previously served twice as Warden.[90]

Stone was regarded as one of the most skilled sculptors and architect/builders in London but notwithstanding his operative eminence he was only 'taken into the Acception' in 1638, by which point he had achieved a position of some affluence via

---

[87] Scanlan, 'Nicholas Stone and the Mystery of the Acception'.
[88] Daily pay rates as per Zachary Babington, *Notice to Grand Jurors* (London, 1677).
[89] Nicholas Stone (1586-1647)
[90] Adam White, 'Nicholas Stone', *ODNB*.

commissions for aristocratic and wealthy clients and patrons that included the Countess of Middlesex,[91] Viscount Dorchester,[92] the Goldsmiths Company,[93] the Earl of Danby[94] and Sir Christopher Hatton.[95]

Knoop and Jones have also put forward an argument that the Acception was a predominantly social forum, observing that the Masons' Company accounts mention the Acception throughout the seventeenth century and that the statements largely detail the sums spent on the Acception's dinners and list the balances owed by members.[96]

A number of entries record the names of those who were admitted as members; that for 1649-50, for example, lists six new entrants, of whom four were members of the Masons' Company. That the

---

[91] Centre for Kentish Studies: U269/A462/5: 1639.
[92] Society of Antiquaries: SAL/MS/263.
[93] John Newman, 'Nicholas Stone's Goldsmiths' Hall: Design and Practice in the 1630s', *Architectural History*, 14 (1971), 30-141.
[94] *Ibid.*
[95] White, 'Nicholas Stone', *ODNB*.
[96] Douglas Knoop and G. P. Jones, *The Genesis of Freemasonry* (London, 1978), pp. 146-7.

two non-members paid an acceptance fee of 40*s*, twice that paid by the Company's working members, is significant and recalls the common guild practice of issuing invitations to membership as an effective form of subsidy. The description also resonates with Ashmole's record of the March 1682 meeting and his observation that dinner was 'prepared at the Charge of the new accepted Masons'.

The Acception declined and ceased to exist some years after the formal incorporation of the London Company of Masons in 1677 and the status of the Company itself waned following the end of its monopoly under Charles II and the restrictions placed on City livery companies more generally by James II.[97]

Although there is an element of elegance in Prescott's comment that 'it is tempting to assume that ... the formation of a Grand Lodge of Free and Accepted Masons was in effect a revival of the

---

[97] Mark Knights, 'A City Revolution: The Remodelling of the London Livery Companies in the 1680s', *English Historical Review*, 112.449 (1997), 1141-78.

Acception',[98] the evidence does not support the parallel.

As with Chester Freemasonry, the membership records of the Ancient Lodge at York – in 1725 renamed the Grand Lodge at York – also point to a high proportion of gentlemen and a leadership intertwined with the city's social, financial and political élite.[99]

Yorkshire Freemasonry was part of a tradition reaching back several centuries. Indeed, had the governance of the Grand Lodge of England in the early eighteenth century been less effective, York may well have been a valid contender for Masonic leadership in Britain. But notwithstanding its longevity and the political weight of York and Yorkshire county politics, there were several reasons why Yorkshire Freemasonry lacked the resonance and influence of London's new Grand Lodge.

The nature and character of its leaders was key. Yorkshire Freemasonry was headed by predominantly

---

[98] Prescott, 'The Old Charges Revisited'.
[99] Cf. Barker Cryer, *York Mysteries Revealed*, pp. 173-218.

Tory politicians, some Catholic, many anti-Hanoverian, whose views sat badly with the king and the London administration. One of the more prominent of York's early eighteenth-century Presidents[100] was Robert Benson,[101] who provides an elegant illustration of lack of influence following the Hanoverian succession post-1714.

Benson was a Tory MP for Thetford and later York, appointed to the Treasury in 1710 under Lord Harley who in 1711 promoted him to Chancellor. Two years later, Benson was elevated to the peerage as Baron Bingley and appointed ambassador to Spain. He was however reportedly disliked by many of his fellow peers[102] and lost office in 1714 after the Hanoverian succession. From that point he was

---

[100] The term 'Grand Master' only came into use in York around 1725 following the formation of the Grand Lodge of England and the appointments of its Grand Masters. The previously adopted form of address was 'President'.

[101] Robert Benson (1676-1731), President of York, hereafter 'PrY', 1707.

[102] D. Hayton, E. Cruickshanks & S. Handley (eds.), *The History of Parliament: the House of Commons 1690-1715* (London, 2002): http://www.historyofparliamentonline.org/volume/1690-1715/member/benson-robert-1676-1731, accessed June 2015.

in opposition and only returned to favour briefly in 1730, a year before his death.[103]

Benson's successor as President of York Freemasonry was Sir William Robinson,[104] Lord Mayor of York in 1700, who sat as MP for Northallerton from 1689 until 1695, and for the City of York from 1698 until 1722.[105] He was followed by Sir Walter Hawksworth,[106] Yorkshire's High Sheriff in 1721, who was succeeded by Sir George Tempest,[107] and then by Charles Fairfax,[108] one of the city's more overt Jacobite sympathisers.

While President of the lodge at York, Fairfax was one of several leading Catholics summoned by the mayor and aldermen of the city and asked to make

---

[103] The Treaty of Seville between Britain, France and Spain concluded the Anglo-Spanish war and paved the way for the Treaty of Vienna the following year. As a reward for his support, Bingley was appointed Treasurer to the Household, a sinecure by Royal Warrant paying c.£1,200 per annum.
[104] Sir William Robinson (1655-1736), PrY, 1708–10.
[105] P.M. Tillot, *A History of the County of York, The City of York* (London, 1961), pp. 240-45.
[106] Sir Walter Hawksworth, (16..?-1735), PrY 1711-2.
[107] Sir George Tempest, (1672-1745), PrY, 1713.
[108] Charles Fairfax, PrY 1714–9.

a declaration of loyalty in favour of the Hanoverian succession and to give up their horses and any arms in their household. Others so summoned included Benson and at least eight other families, some Catholic, all connected to Yorkshire Freemasonry.[109] Fairfax refused to comply. He was fined, imprisoned and released only in November 1715 after the Jacobites had unconditionally surrendered. It is notable that his political allegiances met with local Masonic approval and that Fairfax remained President of York Freemasonry for a further four years.

And Yorkshire Freemasonry was handicapped by other factors. First, where the Grand Lodge of England in London was headed by celebrated aristocratic figureheads and supported by senior civil servants, members of the judiciary, wealthy merchants, eminent soldiers and professional men with influence and connections, all part of the ruling élite, the Ancient Lodge at York was comprised largely of lesser provincial worthies. Second, the Grand Lodge of England was associated with the Enlightenment

---

[109] Barker Cryer, *York Mysteries Revealed*, pp. 226-7.

concepts championed by Martin Clare,[110] John Desaguliers and Martin Folkes, among others.[111] In contrast, Yorkshire Freemasonry lacked the influence that such intellectual imprimatur exerted.

In political and Masonic terms the Ancient Lodge at York was side-lined: 'the new organisation in the South ... under the denomination of the Grand Lodge of England ... on account of its situation, being encouraged by some of the principal nobility, soon acquired consequence and reputation; while [York] ... seemed gradually to decline'.[112]

It could be regarded as ironic that towards the end of the seventeenth century and in the first decade

---

[110] Martin Clare (c.1690-1751), a Justice of the Peace and Master of The Academy in Soho Square, was one of the most influential freemasons in the 1730s. He served as a Grand Steward, Grand Warden and Deputy Grand Master.

[111] Martin Folkes (1690-1754), FRS, a privately wealthy, clubbable intellectual.

[112] The comment was made by the Grand Lodge of York itself. Cf. also Preston, *Illustrations of Masonry*, p. 190. Also, *Masonic Miscellany and Ladies' Literary Magazine* (Lexington, 1822), vol. 1, p. 129.

of the eighteenth, freemasonry had only a limited following in London and the South of England. James Anderson, perhaps the ultimate eighteenth-century apologist for the Craft, noted that 'in the South the Lodges were more and more disused ... and the annual Assembly ... not duly attended'.[113] Anderson did however qualify his comments, writing that although 'particular lodges were not so frequent and mostly occasional in the South', the exception were those located 'in or near the Places where great Works were carried on'.[114]

This was almost certainly an embroidery. Despite Anderson's assertions, there is no independent evidence that suggests the presence of any gentlemanly London lodges whether 'at St Thomas's Hospital', 'in Piccadilly over against St James's Church', 'near Westminster Abbey', 'near Covent Garden', 'in Holborn', 'on Tower-Hill', or elsewhere.[115] And despite Anderson's statements, there is nothing to suggest that 'the king [William of Orange] was privately

---

[113] James Anderson, *The New Book of Constitutions of the Antient and Honourable Fraternity of Free and Accepted Masons* (London, 1738), p. 108.
[114] *Ibid.*, p. 106-7.
[115] *Ibid.*

made a Free Mason' or that he 'approved' of the choice of Wren as Grand Master.

However, although Anderson may have exaggerated their number and nature, there is evidence that Masonic lodges existed in London and the South of England in the early years of the eighteenth century. In addition to the four lodges that founded Grand Lodge in 1717, we can point to the Duke of Richmond's lodge at Chichester and to others.

Economic and social evolution had from the fifteenth century slowly transformed the guilds from quasi-religious orders into embryonic collective bargaining organisations, and their later assimilation into polite society allowed them to become an integral part of the social structure within many English cities.

There is no need to argue whether operative and non-operative freemasonry co-existed in the years before the formation of the Grand Lodge of England - it did. But there was no unbroken thread of ritual and spiritual purpose that joined pre-mediaeval and mediaeval freemasonry to what was to be launched in the early decades of the eighteenth century.

John Pine's
List of Regular Lodges as Constituted 'till March 25th 1725
Frontispiece by Sir James Thornhill

What factors led English Freemasonry to develop so radically from 1717 and into the 1720s?

What motives lay behind the creation of the first Grand Lodge of England? And what were the forces that propelled freemasonry to the high ground of eighteenth-century society?

The answers are complex. And although there were many factors that differentiated eighteenth-century freemasonry from Britain's numerous other clubs and societies, perhaps the most significant was the composition of freemasonry's new leadership.

The Grand Lodge of England was the creation of an inner circle at the Duke of Richmond's Masonic lodge in Westminster. The lodge had met at the Rummer & Grapes in Channel Row before moving in the early 1720s to the nearby Horn Tavern in New Palace Yard. Its members included aristocrats and politicians alongside senior public officials such as Charles Delafaye, an Under Secretary of State and the government's anti-Jacobite spymaster, and William Cowper, a leading magistrate and the Clerk to the Parliaments, the highest ranking administrator at the House of Commons and House of Lords and a nephew of the Lord Chancellor.

Another was the Rev. John Theophilus Desaguliers, arguably the leading figure behind the formation of the new Grand Lodge.[116] Despite having fled France as a child to exile in London, Desaguliers climbed out of poverty to gain an Oxford education and achieve status as a Fellow of the Royal Society[117] and the country's leading consulting engineer. He was also a popular and well-paid public lecturer, described by his lead patron, the Duke of Chandos, as 'the best mechanic in Europe', and more recently as 'arguably the most successful scientific lecturer of the century'.[118]

---

[116] Cf. Berman, *The Foundations of Modern Freemasonry*, esp. chapters two and five.

[117] For biographies of Desaguliers see Berman, *The Foundations of Modern Freemasonry*, esp. chapter two, and Audrey T. Carpenter, *John Theophilus Desaguliers. A Natural Philosopher, Engineer and Freemason in Newtonian England* (London, 2011).

[118] Larry Stewart, 'A Meaning for Machines: Modernity, Utility, and the Eighteenth-Century British Public', *Journal of Modern History*, 70.2 (1998), 259-94, esp. 269; and 'James Brydges to William Mead, 16 June 1718', Huntington Library: Stowe MS, ST 57, XV, 252.

Foundations

Jean Theophilus Desaguliers
Painted by T.R. Beaufort Hinks in 1901 from a 1725
mezzotint by Peter Pelham (*c*.1695-1753)

Under Desaguliers' aegis and with the support of influential colleagues that included George Payne and Martin Folkes, the latter later the President of the Royal Society, and the lesser known Alexander

Chocke,[119] Nathaniel Blackerby,[120] John Beale[121] and George Carpenter,[122] English Freemasonry embraced Enlightenment ideals and religious toleration, and for many became a public statement if not an avowal of pro-Hanoverian conformity.

Desaguliers and Folkes were pivotal in persuading the Duke of Montagu[123] to accept the leadership of the Craft, as was the example of the Duke of Richmond, Montagu's close friend and neighbour.

---

[119] Alexander Chocke (16.?-1737), a Westminster justice and senior civil servant at the Exchequer. Chocke succeeded Cowper as DGM in 1727; he had been GW in 1726.

[120] Nathaniel Blackerby (16..?-1742), another JP and one of Chocke's colleagues at the Exchequer, was DGM in 1728 and 1729. Blackerby was appointed the first Grand Treasurer of Grand Lodge in 1731.

[121] John Beale died on 20 June 1724 at his Berkshire home. He had been appointed DGM in 1721 and elected FRS the same year; his proposer was William Stukeley, whose Masonic initiation he had attended, and Edmund Halley. Beale was responsible with Desaguliers for reviewing the *1723 Constitutions*.

[122] Hon. Colonel George Carpenter (c.1694-1749), later 2nd baron Carpenter of Killaghy, MP for Morpeth (1717-27), GW in 1729.

[123] John, 2nd duke of Montagu (1690-1749), GM 1721.

Montagu's installation as Grand Master marked a turning point. It enhanced freemasonry's ability to attract new members and added to Grand Lodge's authority over the rapidly rising number of lodges being constituted in London and the provinces. Freemasonry's popularity was such that where before 1720 the annual Grand Feast had been held above a tavern, the Goose and Gridiron Alehouse, in 1721 - and with Montagu at the head of the order - Grand Lodge was obliged to relocate the event to the capacious Stationers' Hall in order to avoid disappointing the several hundred and more freemasons who wished to attend.

The publication of a new set of *Constitutions* in 1723 contained a revised set of *Regulations* and *Charges* and introduced positions within Grand Lodge to which Masonic patronage could be applied. Both were key building blocks in what Desaguliers and Payne later developed into a national, then international federal structure.

The *1723 Constitutions* recorded that

several Noblemen and gentlemen of the best rank, with Clergymen and learned scholars of

> *most professions and denominations ... joined and submitted to take the charges ... under our present worthy Grand Master, the most noble Prince, John, Duke of Montagu.*

This was key. Montagu demonstrated that freemasonry was acceptable morally, intellectually and politically - and that it could be fashionable and fun. The combination provided the justification and rationale for those of 'the best rank' and for 'learned scholars of most professions and denominations' to join the Craft.

Freemasonry offered an intriguing mix. Its *Constitutions* supported the state and legitimised its authority and at the same time encouraged, if not demanded, religious tolerance and moral integrity. And Masonic meetings provided not only a genial social setting in which to network and a vaunted emphasis on toasting, drinking and dining, but also antiquarian ritual and an opportunity to benefit from entertaining and educational lectures.

Freemasonry's positive image was burnished by a programme of effective press management as well as aristocratic leadership. Newspapers published

Masonic missives, including digests of Grand Lodge's Quarterly Communications, and Masonic feasts, processions and philanthropy were also reported and lauded accordingly.[124]

Freemasonry had been redesigned to sit above political and social censure: admitting only 'good and true Men, free-born, and of mature and discreet Age, no Bondmen, no Women, no immoral or scandalous men, but of good Report'. And in the second and third decades of the eighteenth century it can be said to have succeeded.

Montagu's social and political status underlines and explains why he was chosen as the Craft's first noble Grand Master. He was intelligent, wealthy and well-connected. And he was pro-Huguenot and a staunch Hanoverian.

Montagu's father, Ralph Montagu, the 1st duke, had been ambassador to Louis XIV of France and had witnessed the persecution of the Huguenots at first hand. He had been described as 'a great

---

[124] Cf. Andrew Pink, *The Musical Culture of Freemasonry in Early Eighteenth-century London* (University College London, unpublished PhD thesis, 2007).

supporter of the French and other Protestants [driven] to England by the tyranny of their princes, [and] an admirer of learning and learned men'.[125] And Montagu's grandmother, Rachel de Massue, had been a Huguenot aristocrat.

Montagu himself had grown up among Huguenots at Boughton Hall, the family's main country estate, and in common with many others among the Whig aristocracy had been educated by Huguenot tutors.[126] Moreover, his close relations included the eminent Huguenot soldier, Henri de Massue, Marquis de Ruvigny, later Earl of Galway.

---

[125] John Macky, *Memoirs of the secret services ... during the reigns of King William, Queen Anne, and King George I* (London, 1733).

[126] Berman, *The Foundations of Modern Freemasonry*, pp. 132-3.

Foundations

John, 2nd Duke of Montagu
Mezzotint by John Faber Jr. after Sir Godfrey Kneller, unknown date

Desaguliers and Folkes recognised Montagu as an ideal figurehead for any society seeking to elevate its status, and Montagu was propelled to the position of Grand Master with the probable intention that his wealth, social standing, Court connections and military rank would act as a beacon to attract others from his circles and elsewhere. And it did.

Montagu's activities featured regularly in the metropolitan and provincial press with close to 300 news reports published between 1721 and 1735, including coverage of his loyal address to George I,[127] position as chief mourner at the funeral of the Duke of Marlborough, his father-in-law,[128] and his eldest daughter's wedding to the Duke of Manchester.[129] Even an excursion along the Thames in a 'large flat bottom boat' was considered worthy of mention;[130] indeed, his appointment as Lord Proprietor and Captain General of St Lucia and St Vincent was reported not only in London and the provinces but as far away as Boston in colonial Massachusetts.[131]

---

[127] *Daily Courant*, 28 July 1722.
[128] His role as chief mourner was endorsed by his mother-in-law, Lady Churchill. Cf. *Daily Journal*, 13 August 1722.
[129] *Freeholder's Journal*, 13 February 1723.
[130] *Universal Spectator and Weekly Journal*, 19 June 1731.
[131] *New England Courant*, 17 September 1722. There was of course an obvious trading interest between the American colonies and the West Indies.

Montagu also had the advantage of a close association with the royal household. He succeeded his father as Master of the Great Wardrobe, a sinecure that paid over £3,000 a year, officiated as Lord High Constable at the coronation of George I in 1714, and in 1727 carried the sceptre at George II's coronation.[132] Montagu also served as Lord Lieutenant of both Northamptonshire and Warwickshire, in each case for life from 1715.[133] And he held prominent military positions and not simply those that were honorific or a consequence of his position as Marlborough's son-in-law.

Montagu politicked actively to be appointed to the right roles. In a reference to his request for the governorship of the Isle of Wight, Montagu commented that he wanted it badly that he might 'again … be a military man, that being a military post'.[134] He also raised and financed regiments of Horse and Foot, and was later captain and colonel

---

[132] Edward Charles Metzger, 'John Montagu, 2nd Duke of Montagu', *ODNB*.
[133] *London Gazette*, 2 July 1715.
[134] *John Montagu, letter to Robert Walpole*, quoted in Jacob, *The Radical Enlightenment*, p. 102. The original is at CUL: Chol. MSS 2008, 5 July 1734.

of His Majesty's Own Troop of Horse Guards, the army's premier cavalry regiment.

In Montagu's wake and with the support and encouragement of the Duke of Richmond, other often young and wealthy aristocrats were encouraged to take the chair at Grand Lodge and to give their imprimatur by associating publicly with the Craft. Such recommendations provided a further spur to the expansion of freemasonry into the gentry, the military, the professions and, perhaps most significantly, among the aspirational middling. The move catapulted Grand Lodge and London Freemasonry into the public consciousness and created what became within only a few years a fashionable club whose aspiring members could consider, probably justifiably, that they were on the inside of one of the sets that mattered.

Nonetheless there was a setback - the election of the Duke of Wharton as Grand Master in 1722.[135] Wharton had been made a freemason only a few months after Montagu had been installed as Grand

---

[135] Philip, Duke of Wharton (1698-1731).

Master. As *Applebee's Original Weekly Journal* noted on 5 August 1721,

> *the Ceremonies being performed at the King's Arms Tavern ... His Grace [Wharton] came Home to his House in the Pall-Mall in a white Leathern Apron.*

Mercurial and self-interested, Wharton usurped rather than succeeded Montagu as Grand Master as he sought either to commandeer what was perceived as a potentially influential organisation, or merely cause a nuisance.

Regardless of his motives and perhaps because of his status and wealth, Wharton was accepted as Grand Master - reluctantly or otherwise - and Desaguliers and other loyal Whigs were present at the feast on 25 June 1722 that marked his installation.[136]

---

[136] *Compleat Set of St James's Journals*, 28 June 1722 *et al.*

Philip, Duke of Wharton
Unknown Artist, c.1722.

A report of the meeting in the *London Journal* of 30 June 1722 noted that membership of the Society was then some 4,000. If accurate, and it may not have been, this would have been an astonishing achievement, representing almost a third of London's gentry and upper middling men.

Wharton's appointment was nonetheless divisive and his insistence that the musicians at dinner play the Jacobite song 'Let the King enjoy his own again' was an obvious and petty anti-Hanoverian display:

Then let us rejoice, With heart and voice,
There doth one Stuart still remain;
And all sing the tune, On the tenth day of June,
That the King shall enjoy his own again

Such a political statement would have been considered offensive by many if not most of those present. In Pope's words, Wharton was 'a fool, with more of wit than half mankind, too rash for thought, for action too refined'.[137]

Wharton was reprimanded accordingly by Desaguliers and 'Hanoverian decorum was restored, toasts were drunk to prosperity under the present Administration, and to Love, Liberty, and Science'.[138]

---

[137] Alexander Pope, *Epistle to Cobham* (London, 1734).
[138] David Stevenson, 'James Anderson: Man & Mason', *Heredom*, 10 (2002), 93-138.

Regardless, Wharton remained unpopular with the Whig majority in Grand Lodge and his and his followers' exodus a year later in June 1723 cemented the pro-Hanoverian nature of the Craft under the Duke of Richmond, John Desaguliers and their associates.

Wharton's effective expulsion occurred the same week that he defended Francis Atterbury, the Jacobite Bishop of Rochester, against a charge of treason. And despite Atterbury's censure, Wharton accompanied Atterbury for part of his journey into exile and brazenly provided him with the gift of an engraved sword.[139]

This was not an image that Grand Lodge would have wanted to project onto English Freemasonry, nor one with which senior freemasons would wish to be associated. The flourish with which Desaguliers signed the Minutes that recorded Wharton's

---

[139] Cf. *Weekly Journal or Saturday's Post*, 22 June 1723; *British Journal*, 29 June 1723; and *London Journal*, 29 June 1723.

departure 'without ceremony' from Grand Lodge was undertaken with feeling.[140]

Wharton's attempt to turn the Craft towards the Jacobites and against the Hanoverian administration had been rebuffed and he had been removed. He was replaced in the chair by the Earl of Dalkeith, a malleable and loyal government supporter. John Desaguliers was named his Deputy Grand Master, exercising power in Dalkeith's name.

Wharton's reign and Dalkeith's succession consolidated Desaguliers and his colleagues' influence over freemasonry. A stream of centralising regulations were issued designed to minimise the risk of future radical change. Many of such rules remain in place including one of the best known Masonic edicts, passed in Grand Lodge in January 1723, which confirmed that 'it was not in the power of any body of men to make any Alteration or Innovation in the body of Masonry without the consent first obtained of the Annual Grand Lodge'.

---

[140] *Grand Lodge Minutes* were usually signed by the presiding Grand Master at the next regular meeting of Grand Lodge. In this instance they were signed by Desaguliers.

Freemasonry's fourth Grand Master, the Duke of Richmond, an even more celebrated aristocrat, reinforced the Craft's pro-Hanoverian nature. As with Montagu, Richmond's life was the subject of considerable public interest. Over 600 press articles concerning the duke and his family were published during the ten-year period from his father's death in May 1723 to June 1733, and more than 2,300 other entries in later years.

Foundations

Charles Lennox, 2nd Duke of Richmond & Lennox
Portrait by Jonathan Richardson ((1665-1745), *c*.1724

Although Richmond ranked below Montagu in terms of wealth he was an eminent and popular member of the aristocracy and, within Sussex, a prominent and politically valuable politician[141]

---

[141] Timothy McCann, *Correspondence of the Dukes of Richmond and Newcastle* (Lewes, 1984), pp. xxiii-xxx.

connected to both the Duke of Newcastle and Sir Robert Walpole, the Prime Minister. Like Montagu, he also had strong links to the learned and professional societies, including the Royal Society, where Martin Folkes was then a Vice President. Not coincidentally, Folkes served as Richmond's Deputy Grand Master.

Richmond also collaborated extensively with Desaguliers, convening lodges in Paris and at his country estate at d'Aubigny in France as vehicles for Masonic proselytising and British political diplomacy.

Montagu, Richmond and others at Grand Lodge shared a common outlook shaped by successive European wars and the political and religious upheaval that followed England's Glorious Revolution of 1688.

The Glorious Revolution may have swept William and Mary to the British throne and in 1702 secured Queen Anne as their successor, but it failed to void the threat posed by James Francis

Foundations

Edward Stuart – the exiled 'king over the water' - whose entitlement to rule as James III of England and James VIII of Scotland was considered by many to be valid.

James Stuart's supporters and allies included not only France, Spain and other European monarchies, but also a minority of English and Scots, Protestant and Catholic, who held the Hanoverian succession to be illegitimate and James Stuart to be Britain's true constitutional monarch. Indeed, even after the crushing of the 1715 Jacobite rebellion, the Stuarts' dynastic claims retained sufficient traction for them to be pursued for another three decades, not least by Charles Stuart - 'Bonnie Prince Charlie' - James' charismatic son, in conjunction with his European and domestic allies.

The existential threat posed by the Jacobites to Whig political supremacy in England and to the Hanoverian line was genuine as well as imagined, and it did not dissipate until the Jacobite danger finally disintegrated in the wake of the 1745 uprising.

Anti-Jacobite fear drove many aspects of British life, not simply government policy, and it was a powerful implicit and explicit influence on English Freemasonry and on Grand Lodge.

The threat posed to Britain by the return of a Catholic Stuart monarch and Catholicism was part of a battle for religious supremacy in Europe that dated back to the mid-sixteenth century.

In France, the conflict had been expressed in more than a century of persecution of its Huguenot minority, members of John Calvin's Protestant Reformed Church,[142] who were viewed by the French Catholic hierarchy and by Rome as heretics.

There was little practical distinction between the state and the established Catholic Church and a threat to one was considered a danger to the other. Because of its wealth and influence from the pulpit, the Church was vitally important. It wielded a defining influence in rural and urban communities, and its central doctrine of fealty to king and church was positioned as a fundamental –

---

[142] John Calvin (1509-1564).

indeed, integral – component of the natural God-ordained order.

The rise of Calvinism caused a religious stand-off between Catholicism and the new Protestantism and resulted in the unrelenting oppression of the Huguenots.

From the 1550s there was close to four decades of internecine religious war within France. Two of many examples give an indication of the scale of conflict: *Vassy*, where on 1 March 1562 some 1,200 Huguenots were slaughtered; and the *St Bartholomew's Day Massacre* of 23 August 1572, when some 8,000 Huguenots were murdered in Paris with some estimates suggesting that up to 90,000 were killed elsewhere in France.

The massacre was celebrated in Paris and in Rome, and thanksgiving prayers were ordered to be said to thank God for having 'granted the Catholic people a glorious triumph'.[143] England's ambassador to the French Court at the time was Sir Francis

---

[143] Russell Jacoby, *Bloodlust: On the Roots of Violence from Cain and Abel to the Present* (New York, 2011), p. 8.

Walsingham, later Queen Elizabeth's spymaster, and his first-hand experience of the persecution of the Huguenots did much to reinforce both his and England's anti-Catholic and pro-Huguenot disposition.

Henry IV's Edict of Nantes in April 1598 sought to lessen the religious conflict and attempted to introduce a different perspective to the relationship between church and state. Henry IV had been born a Huguenot but on succeeding to the French throne had taken a pragmatic approach and converted to Catholicism. Some 85% of France's population was Catholic and Henry needed the support of the Catholic Church to rule. However although the Edict gave the Huguenots a degree of religious freedom, it did not usher in religious tolerance but rather entrenched the Catholic establishment, confining the Huguenots to enclaves where they could be controlled and neutralized.

Henry IV was murdered in 1610 and Huguenot oppression resumed under Louis XIII and was expanded under Louis XIV, who assumed power personally after 1661. The siege of La Rochelle in 1628, with the death of some three-fifths of the city's 28,000 population, and the razing of almost three-quarters of France's 800 Protestant churches in the three decades to 1685, are only two of many examples of Huguenot persecution.

Under Louis XIV's guiding principle of 'one Faith, one Law, one King', Huguenot maltreatment became entrenched state policy. And it arguably reached a peak in the early and mid-1680s with the introduction of the *Dragonnades*, the forced billeting of French dragoons on Huguenot households that became synonymous with violence, rape and theft. Capping this, in 1685 the Edict of Nantes was revoked and the limited protections that it had offered were removed.

In response, Huguenot emigration from France accelerated. Almost a third of France's Huguenot population fled, an estimated 200-250,000 people.[144] Some 50,000 left for England with the balance settling in the Low Countries, the German states and Switzerland, with a smaller proportion

---

[144] The total French population at the time was around 18 million. To put that figure into perspective, England's population was barely more than 5 million.

migrating to Southern Africa and North America, especially South Carolina.[145]

Of those who journeyed to England, the majority eventually settled in London. There they joined an existing Huguenot community, itself the product of flight over the preceding century. The new influx had a substantial impact. London's population in the 1690s was around 450,000 and the entry of so many Huguenot refugees represented around 10% of the enlarged population.

Although British government policy was generally protective and supportive of the French émigrés, and despite their being nominally safe in a Protestant country, Britain's Huguenot émigrés nonetheless feared for their long term security. Conflict with France and Spain remained a particular threat. And notwithstanding that the negotiations that preceded the signing of the peace treaty at Utrecht in 1713 had aroused hope in the Huguenot diaspora that the Protestant powers might exert influence on Louis XIV to roll back religious persecution in

---

[145] Robin Gwynn, *Huguenot Heritage* (Brighton, 2001), 2nd revised edn., pp. 29-30.

France, such a development was not to be. Henri de Mirmand, the Swiss Huguenot who acted as their advocate, was unsuccessful, writing to London's French churches in June 1713 to advise of his failure and to recommend patience.[146]

Matters deteriorated further when eighteen months later in 1715 the Huguenots and the newly installed George I and his Whig ministry came under direct threat from what Lord Galway termed 'de l'invasion d'un prétendant papist', the invasion of the Papist Pretender, the Jacobite Rising, with the terrifying possibility that a Catholic monarch might be reinstated in Britain.

The Hanoverian establishment and the Huguenots took the Jacobite threat seriously. In a letter to the West Street Church Lord Galway asked apprehensively 'combien il y auroit de gens de votre église capables de prendre les armes en cas de nécessité' - how many from the Huguenot community might be able to take up arms if required. And with the government concerned about the possibility of papist spies,

---

[146] William & Susan Minet, *Registres des Quatres Eglises du Petit Charenton de West Street de Pearl Street et de Crispin Street* (London, 1929), vol. XXXII, p. xv.

London's French churches were instructed to monitor and report on any new members seeking to be admitted to their congregation.[147]

Religious and political insecurity would remain a constant theme within Britain's Huguenot community across the following decades. Notwithstanding the setback to the Jacobite cause in 1715, four years later, James Stuart and his supporters found new allies in Count Giulio Alberoni, a Cardinal and a leading minister to Philip V of Spain, and in Charles XII of Sweden and his senior ministers and overseas ambassadors. The subsequent Spanish-backed attempt at invasion in 1722 alongside a putative Jacobite uprising in Scotland wove fear deeper into the Huguenot psyche and reinforced the Huguenots' loyalty to the Hanoverian succession and to successive Whig administrations.

These fears were reflected in English Freemasonry. The anti-Jacobite, pro-Hanoverian loyalties of

---

[147] Minet, *Registres des Quatres Eglises du Petit Charenton de West Street de Pearl Street et de Crispin Street*, p. xvi.

its Whig and Huguenot leaders gave freemasonry traction with the establishment. And the support was mutual. Implicit government backing allowed London's Grand Lodge to become the centre of English Freemasonry and to extend its jurisdiction from London to key provincial cities and, over time, much of England and Wales.

The inner core of London Freemasonry, the Deputy Grand Master and other grand officers, and the masters and senior members of an élite circle of influential Masonic lodges, the Horn Tavern, the Rummer, the Bedford Head and King's Arms foremost among them, comprised parliamentarians, senior civil servants, military officers, the gentry, and eminent professional men and intellectuals.

Importantly, many were also government-appointed magistrates; indeed, at least twenty-three members of the Horn, close to a third of its reported membership, sat on the Middlesex and Westminster benches.[148] One of the most senior was Charles Delafaye, a long-serving Under Secretary of State and the government's most trusted anti-Jacobite

---

[148] Berman, *Schism*, p. 115.

spymaster. Indeed, four members of the Horn Tavern lodge served as Chairman of either or both the Middlesex and Westminster magistrates' benches: William Cowper; Alexander Chocke; Nathaniel Blackerby; and Leonard Streate.[149]

While there is no evidence to support the suggestion that the relationship between freemasonry and the judiciary was interdependent, or that there was a government or Masonic conspiracy to crowd the bench with freemasons, it is reasonable to conclude that many freemasons represented precisely the type of men that the government favoured.

The changes made to the composition of the magistracy from 1714 were substantive.[150] Successive Hanoverian Lord Chancellors were rigorous in appointing dependable political allies and removing potential opposition Tories and Jacobite sympathisers. This was above all the case in the ultra-sensitive areas of Westminster and Middlesex where the bench was configured to be explicitly supportive of the

---

[149] Leonard Streate (16..?-1729).
[150] Norma Landau, 'Country Matters: The Growth of Political Stability a Quarter Century On', *Albion*, 25.2 (1993), 261-74.

London administration. In a memorable phrase, 'fidelity to the Hanoverian [government was] a touchstone for fitness'.[151]

Supporting this analysis but not mentioned by historians, the first three Hanoverian Lord Chancellors - William Cowper, the 1st Earl Cowper, Lord Chancellor from 1714 to 1718; Thomas Parker, the 1st Earl of Macclesfield, who succeeded in 1718 and remained in post until 1725; and Peter King, the 1st Baron King of Ockham, who sat from 1725 until 1733 - all had strong family connections with freemasonry. Earl Cowper's nephews included William Cowper, the pivotal Grand Secretary and Deputy Grand Master, and his brother, the Rev. John Cowper, a fellow member of the Horn. The Earl of Macclesfield's son, George Parker, who later succeeded to the title, was a member of the Duke of Richmond's lodge at the Swan in Chichester, as was William Jones, also a member of the Queen's Head in Hollis Street, a close friend to both father and son. And Lord King's son, John, the 2nd Baron

---

[151] Norma Landau, *Justices of the Peace 1679-1760*, (Berkeley, CA, 1984) p. 88.

Ockham, a Grand Steward in 1731, is recorded as a member of the Lodge of Antiquity.[152]

The influence and power of the magistracy was significant and the justice of the peace 'occupied a pivotal position in eighteenth-century England'.[153] Their work did not merely incorporate 'the preservation of the king's peace and justice'. The magistracy also determined the legal seriousness of offences brought before the bench and therefore the appropriate type – and thus severity - of punishment. And in London their role went further. The magistracy was regarded and acted as the principal line of defence against the London mob, and the Grand Jury at the Quarter Sessions pronounced on allegations of all offences, including treason.[154]

---

[152] *Grand Lodge Minutes*, p. 142, fn. (a).

[153] P.B. Munsche, 'Review: The Justice of the Peace, 1679-1760', *Eighteenth Century Studies*, 20.3 (1987), 385-7.

[154] Norma Landau, 'Indictment for Fun and Profit', *Law and History Review*, 17.3 (1999), 507-36; and Robert B. Shoemaker, 'The London Mob in the Early Eighteenth Century', *Journal of British Studies*, 26.3 (1987), 273-304.

Foundations

Senior Warden, *c.*1730
Artist unknown

The support and encouragement of freemasonry and the new Grand Lodge by successive administrations was a product of its pro-establishment and pro-Hanoverian stance and the positive functions that it fulfilled. The characteristics of those at its head, especially senior magistrates such as Cowper,

Delafaye, Blackerby and Thomas De Veil,[155] reinforced the relationship, as did the social arc from which the magistracy - and senior freemasons - was selected.[156]

Charles Delafaye, one of the administration's most important and influential civil servants, was appointed a magistrate in 1714 or 1715 and remained on the bench for more than two decades.[157] His dependability was such that he became one of the government's principal 'go to' figures for political cases.[158] He adjudicated on hearings that ranged from the committal of a Jacobite sympathiser 'for publicly affirming in St James's Park that the Pretender was the only rightful and lawful King'[159] and examining a printer suspected of 'printing the

---

[155] Thomas de Veil (1684-1746).

[156] Landau, *Justices of the Peace 1679-1760*, esp. pp. 69-95, 96-145 and 146-73.

[157] Charles Delafaye's name is recorded in the London & Metropolitan Archives ('LMA') Middlesex Sessions, Sessions Papers, Justices' Working Papers for April 1715: LMA: MJ/SP *1715*. Delafaye also sat on the City of London and City of Westminster benches.

[158] Cf., among many reported examples, *Country Journal or The Craftsman*, 17 November 1733.

[159] *Original Weekly Journal*, 31 August 1717.

libels dispersed in Westminster Hall',[160] to investigating plots against the crown - 'persons who were talking of some misfortune that should happen to the King tomorrow as his Majesty should pass over Sandy End Bridge on his way to London'.[161]

Delafaye was also one of those selected to take part in the Quarter Sessions. That of December 1722, for example, saw him sitting alongside ten other magistrates[162] of whom at least six (and possibly seven) were fellow freemasons.

Nathaniel Blackerby, William Cowper, Charles Delafaye, Alexander Hardine and Francis Sorrel were members of the Horn Tavern lodge; Sir Thomas Jones a member of the Bedford Head; William Vaughan possibly a member of the Rummer; and Joseph Hayne[s] a member of the Royal Vine Yard lodge in St James's.[163]

---

[160] *Old Whig or The Consistent Protestant*, 29 July 1736.
[161] LMA: Middlesex Sessions Papers, Justices' Working Documents, *27 October1731: Information of William Steele of St Clements Danes in the County of Middlesex...*
[162] LMA: Middlesex Sessions, *6 December 1722*.
[163] Berman, *The Foundations of Modern Freemasonry*, esp. chapters three and four.

And since data on Masonic membership is limited with less than two-thirds of members' names recorded in the early 1720s, it is possible that a number of other magistrates present at that and other Quarter Sessions were also freemasons.

These were men who epitomised English Freemasonry's Whig loyalties and their presence in the lodge and on the bench provided confirmation to any doubter that the Craft could and should legitimately be regarded as politically steadfast.

Freemasonry also exerted a spiritual attraction for many of its members, including Delafaye. However he also used the Craft for work-related purposes: to advance government foreign policy and to collect domestic and foreign intelligence, most especially via the Secret Department of the Post Office, an organisation responsible for intercepting, deciphering and transcribing diplomatic and other mail.

The Secret Department reported through Delafaye to the Secretaries of State and from 1718 was run by John Lefevre, like Delafaye, a Huguenot émigré. He was also a fellow freemason, a member of the King's Head lodge in Pall Mall.

The magistracy and the government's association with freemasonry gave the organisation a judicial and political imprimatur that was reinforced by many instances of *de facto* official endorsement. Prominent examples include the raising of the Duke of Lorraine and the initiation of the Duke of Newcastle at Houghton Hall in 1731, and the initiation of other senior figures, including Prime Minister Robert Walpole, Frederick, Prince of Wales, and numerous members of both Court and Parliament.[164]

But although such events provide a clear illustration of freemasonry's political ascent and diplomatic usage, there are other less well-known examples that are of equal significance.

They include the initiation in 1733 of Prince Esterházy at the French Lodge at the Duke of

---

[164] Many of Walpole's press apologists were also freemasons: James Pitt, a member of Folkes' Bedford Head lodge; Raphael Courteville, a member of the lodge at the George, Charing Cross; Lord Hervey, the Queen's Head, Bath; and Theobald Cibber, the Bear & Harrow. Cf, Berman, *The Foundations of Modern Freemasonry*, esp. chapter 3; Simon Targett, 'Government and Ideology during the Age of Whig Supremacy', *Historical Journal*, 37.2 (1994), 289-317; and Targett, 'James Pitt (fl.1744-55)', *ODNB*.

Lorraine's Head, a lodge which had met formerly at the close by Prince Eugene's Coffee House in St James's:

> *On Tuesday last Prince Anthony Esterházy, lately arrived here, and another German Nobleman, a relative to the Elector of Mentz, were admitted Free and Accepted Masons at the French Lodge, held the first and third Tuesday of every Month, at the Duke of Lorraine's Head in Suffolk Street.* [165]

Esterházy was His Serene Highness Prince Paul II Anton Esterházy de Galántha,[166] a Hungarian nobleman and an influential figure at the Habsburg Court in Vienna. The family's estates were vast. The Esterházys were the largest landowners in Hungary with holdings that exceeded 1,850 square miles (4,800 square kilometres), or 5% of Hungary's land mass. Their wealth at the time rivalled that of the

---

[165] *Daily Advertiser*, 9 August 1733.
[166] Prince Paul II Anton Esterházy de Galántha (1711-1762).

House of Habsburg, Holy Roman Emperors from the fifteenth century to the eighteenth.[167]

The reason Esterházy was in London is not certain but would almost certainly have been linked to the Duke of Lorraine's visit two years earlier in 1731, and to the breaking War of the Polish Succession (1733-5) and the move by France and Spain against Austria and the Holy Roman Empire, with France seizing the Duchy of Lorraine and Spain the kingdoms of Naples and Sicily.

Internal political opposition and economic pressures had obliged Britain's support for the Holy Roman Empire to be muted, although a large British fleet was kept on station in the Baltic to forestall an attack from the north. And with the Dutch choosing to remain neutral, Austria and its allies feared isolation. In this context, a private Austrian-Hungarian diplomatic envoy to Britain to seek assurances would have been both natural and understandable.

---

[167] Also known as the House of Hapsburg or House of Austria.

Esterházy spoke French and German but had only a limited knowledge of English. However language alone would not have guided Esterházy to the French Lodge at the Duke of Lorraine's Head. There were other lodges, including the Horn Tavern, that could have accommodated French speakers and whose members were aristocrats. It is therefore more probable that he was directed specifically to the French Lodge, something that would have been effected through private diplomatic channels and thus ultimately through Charles Delafaye as Under Secretary acting on behalf of the Duke of Newcastle, the Secretary of State.

The nobleman accompanying Esterházy to the French Lodge, "another German Nobleman, a relative to the Elector of Mentz' [Mainz], was similarly of political significance.

The Electorate of Mainz was the largest ecclesiastical province in Germany and the most prestigious of the states that made up the Holy Roman Empire. Indeed, its ruler, the Archbishop-Elector, one of seven prince-electors, ranked second in political status behind the Emperor. The Archbishop-Elector also held the title of Arch Chancellor of the Holy Roman Empire and was Germany's primate. He was also responsible for convening and supervising the Electoral College that chose and invested the Holy Roman Emperor.

The presence in London of a close relative and confidential envoy of the Elector - and his association with Esterházy - is a strong indication that the Holy Roman Empire was seeking tangible military and diplomatic support from Britain, or at least assurances. Although it has not been possible to uncover firm evidence of a meeting between Esterhazy and Walpole's ministers in Britain's National Archives, a private meeting at a lodge whose members comprised politically loyal Huguenots, at least some of whom were in government service, would have kept any discussion confidential and substantially excluded from the public domain.

As a footnote, the War of the Polish Succession was ended by the Treaty of Vienna in 1735, a settlement agreed shortly after Esterházy's return to Vienna where he assumed a senior position at the Habsburg Court.

Frontispiece, Cole's *1731 Constitutions*

Conclusion

By the late 1720s, English Freemasonry had become one of - if not the - most attractive yet accessible destinations for the Whig aristocracy, gentry and aspirational middling. Grand Lodge and English Freemasonry's more eminent constituent lodges were led by a parade of noble Grand Masters from John, Duke of Montagu, to Thomas, Duke of Norfolk, Grand Marshall of England.

Freemasonry had been positioned intentionally at the pinnacle of Hanoverian society. And Desaguliers and his colleagues deployed its celebrated social connections, Masonic patronage and a well-managed decades-long publicity campaign to cement an alliance with the British establishment.

For some three decades through to the mid-eighteenth century, the leadership at Grand Lodge was motivated by a powerful desire to support and safeguard the Hanoverian succession. The Whigs and Huguenots at its head believed it to be essential that Britain remain a bulwark against both Jacobitism and the risk of encroachment by continental Europe's absolutist monarchies. And to that end English Freemasonry was positioned in a supporting role.

As a measure of its achievement, the number of lodges within the jurisdiction of the Grand Lodge of England increased from the founding four in 1717 to over sixty in 1725, more than one hundred in 1730 and around two hundred in 1740. And although some lodges failed to survive, by the mid-1730s, Freemasonry under the jurisdiction of the Grand Lodge of England had a presence across London and provincial England and Wales, and internationally from the eastern seaboard of the Americas - Boston, New York, Philadelphia, Charles Town and Savannah - to Bengal in India.

The 300th anniversary of the founding of the first Grand Lodge of England is an opportunity not only for celebration but also to reflect on the many threads that gave rise to that event and created the foundations on which modern Freemasonry stands.

The Library & Museum of Freemasonry

The Library & Museum of Freemasonry is situated in central London at Freemasons' Hall, a location that has been at the centre of English Freemasonry for some 230 years. Completed in 1933, the structure is considered one of the finest examples of British art deco architecture and is the headquarters of the United Grand Lodge of England, the successor organisation to the oldest Grand Lodge in the world. It is also the meeting place for over 1,000 Masonic lodges.

A registered charity, the Library & Museum of Freemasonry is one of the world's leading, largest and most important repositories of historical material concerning eighteenth, nineteenth and twentieth-century freemasonry. It provides a key archive and unique reference source for academic and historical research.

The museum's collections were awarded Designated Status by Britain's Museums, Libraries and Archives Council in 2007 and are recognised widely as being of national and international significance.

The purpose of the Museum & Library is expressed in clear terms in its Deed of Trust:

> *To collect, preserve, conserve, display and make available to enquirers the archives, records, printed material, regalia, jewels and artefacts of Freemasonry and the continued running of a library and museum for the benefit of the general public and making the items available for research and education and the preservation of the items as collections.*

The Library conserves a comprehensive collection of original manuscripts and printed books on almost every facet of English Freemasonry, as well as documentary material on Freemasonry elsewhere and associated subjects, including Masonic music and poetry.

The Museum comprises an extensive permanent assembly of objects linked to Freemasonry including pottery, glassware, porcelain, silver, furniture, textiles, clocks, jewels and regalia, as well as items belonging to celebrated freemasons such as Winston Churchill and Edward VII. They are displayed alongside the Museum's collection of prints and engravings, photographs and Masonic ephemera.

The collection explores the different ranks, offices and branches of Freemasonry and explains some of the symbolism used. It also examines Masonic dining, freemasonry abroad, and freemasonry during wartime, and outlines the purpose and nature of Masonic charities. And it contains a number of exhibits relating to other, non-Masonic fraternal societies.

Exhibitions portraying the history of freemasonry in England and specific aspects of Masonic life are staged on a regular basis.

Part of the catalogue and a guide to research resources is available online at *www.freemasonry.london.museum*.

The Museum is open to the public daily from 10.00 a.m. to 5.00 p.m. and guided tours are held several times per day. Admission is free of charge.

In addition to its educational and research functions, the Library & Museum is the repository for the archives of the United Grand Lodge of England and the Supreme Grand Chapter of England and their predecessor bodies.

The Archive Collections also include historical papers relating to buildings and sites associated with freemasonry, charitable bodies associated with freemasonry, individual freemasons, correspondence, research papers, and a substantial number of eighteenth and nineteenth century lodge and chapter records, including Minute books, Treasurers' accounts and attendance and other membership records, many of which give the name, address, age and occupation of members.

The Document Collection includes Masonic patents of appointment, certificates, warrants and charters; and the Print Collection photographs, engravings and prints of a wide range of freemasons in addition to Masonic events and subjects.

The Grand Lodge of England (established in 1717) and the Antients Grand Lodge (established in 1751) both maintained registers of their members and each retained important correspondence. This was generally held in secure boxes (several are recorded as being made), and were kept, in the case of the Grand Lodge of England, in one of the rooms maintained for the use of the Grand Secretary and the various committees. The Articles of Union of 25 November 1813 between the Moderns (the original Grand Lodge of England) and the Antients refer to depositing the new Great Seal of the United Grand Lodge 'in the archives'. At this time Grand Lodge had limited other material apart from the portraits of the Grand Masters that hung on the walls of the Hall, chairs, the Sword of State donated by the Duke of Norfolk, bibles and the Ark of the Masonic Covenant used in meetings of the Grand Lodge.

A proposal to consider 'the mode of forming, preserving and regulating a Masonic Library and Museum' was agreed by Grand Lodge on 6 September 1837 following a report by the recently installed Grand Superintendent of Works, Philip Hardwick, concerning the possible use of the houses at 62 and 63 Great Queen Street. With this additional space available for expansion, it was announced in Grand Lodge on 7 March 1838 that 'the room on the ground floor and on one side of the passage in the House No. 63 appears to be well calculated for the present purposes of a Masonic Museum and Library' and that 'a sum of money not exceeding £100 be placed at the disposal of the Board [for] the purpose of providing for the reception of books, manuscripts and objects of Masonic interest, and for commencing the formation of the Library and Museum'.

The first donation comprised a bound four-volume set of *The Freemasons' Quarterly Review* and a call for further donations resulted in the receipt of some eighty volumes. Grand Lodge subsequently appointed the two joint Grand Secretaries as *ex-officio* curators and by 1840 the Library held some 250 books and manuscripts.

Nonetheless, despite what appears to have been positive initial interest, progress in creating a Library and Museum was not rapid. One of the junior clerks in the Grand Secretary's office, a keen collector, was appointed to work in this first Library & Museum. His obituary in the *Freemason's Quarterly Review* of June 1842 reflected the lack of evolution: 'he arranged the few books and manuscripts in the Masonic library, and had the contributions to this department been ever so extensive, he would have been delighted to have regulated them; as it was, he considered the office of curator as disgraceful, having nothing to do'.

A move at Grand Lodge in 1847 by John Royston Scarborough supported by Robert Crucefix to secure an annual £20 grant to the Library & Museum was withdrawn after a speech from the Grand Master, the Earl of Zetland, suggested that £20 was insufficient and that they would need a Librarian 'of great skill and high education to be constantly on the premises'. Unfortunately, the cost - some £150 per annum - was more than Grand Lodge could afford.

Scarborough's action prompted the Grand Lodge's Board of General Purposes to report on the state of the collections. It noted that the Library owned 279 books on freemasonry and other subjects, a series of printed lists of lodges and calendars dating back to 1723, Court Directories and six atlases. The report also noted that only £56 9*s* 6*d* of the original £100 grant had been spent.

Notwithstanding, the Library & Museum's premises in No. 63 had by now become inadequate and the Board recommended a move to the anteroom of Sir John Soane's Temple. The first Library regulations were proposed, including regular opening times on Tuesdays, Thursdays and Saturdays from 2 p.m. until 8 p.m., readers being required to sign a visitors' book, a rule that no books should leave the Library, and that the Grand Tyler should be in attendance to deliver books to readers and return them to the shelves, for which he would receive an extra £15 a year. It was also proposed that a catalogue should be produced from the remainder of the £100 grant and that this would be available to members at 6*d*, and that the *Quarterly Communication* of Grand Lodge should note when the Library was open and invite more donations. Scarborough welcomed the report believing that 'great good would be conferred on Masonry by the Library' and its recommendations were passed. Some of the same regulations remain in force today.

In their plans for the redevelopment of the site, the 1862 Building Committee proposed the creation of a Coffee Room and Library that was to be available to subscribers on payment of an annual fee. And in June 1880 Grand Lodge agreed to give the Library & Museum an annual grant of £25 to be spent on preservation, binding and acquiring further books.

The appointment in 1887 of the Grand Tyler, Henry Sadler, as Sub-Librarian inaugurated a period of major change for the Library & Museum. Although the Grand Secretary was still *ex-officio* Librarian and Curator, Sadler's salary was increased by £20 per year to attend the Library, and its opening hours were extended to 10 p.m. on Mondays and Thursdays.

Sadler was the epitome of diligence. He organised and collected archive material, much of which was used as the basis for his own research and that of other members of Quatuor Coronati Lodge, No. 2076, the first lodge of Masonic research. Robert

Freke Gould, the prolific Masonic historian and a fellow member of Quatuor Coronati Lodge, remarked of Sadler that 'scarcely a single Masonic book would have been written without the author being assisted by him'.

When Sadler retired as Grand Tyler in 1910 he was appointed Librarian and Curator on a full time basis with an annual salary of £150, the sum the Earl of Zetland had suggested in 1847. He died just a year later. Sadler had produced two catalogues of the Library Collection, the first in 1888 and the second in 1895. The latter was virtually double the length of the former and is an indication of the growth of the collection during Sadler's time in office.

The formation of Quatuor Coronati Lodge in 1884 and the growth in Masonic historiography that was encouraged and supported by Sadler's work greatly increased interest in the Library & Museum and its collection of Masonic artefacts and books, and lists of donations and acquisitions began to appear in Grand Lodge's *Quarterly Communication* from 1893. The Museum's other collections also continued to grow and were displayed properly for the first time in the new extension of the Hall created by Henry Florence after 1900.

The rules for the architectural competition for the design of Freemasons' Hall - the Masonic Peace Memorial Building - in 1925 included instructions to provide space for a more substantial Library & Museum incorporating a gallery, two Librarians' rooms, a workroom, two strong rooms, a large museum space with good lighting and a separate reading room. Ashley and Newman's winning design placed the Library & Museum on the first floor of the building, the same level as the ceremonial areas. The dedicated space enabled the Library & Museum to develop further into one of the largest and most significant Masonic Collections in the world.

2017 marks the 300th anniversary of the formation of the first Grand Lodge of England, and 2018 the 180th anniversary of the founding of the Library & Museum, which continues to be engaged in a development programme designed to enhance access to the collections through improved cataloguing and via digitisation. The profits from this book support their efforts.

Friends of the Library & Museum

If you wish to support the Library & Museum by joining the 'Friends', please write to the Director at the address below.

Library & Museum of Freemasonry
Freemasons' Hall
60 Great Queen Street
London WC2B 5AZ

Telephone:
+44 (0)20 7395 9257

Email:
libmus@ugle.org.uk

Website:
www.freemasonry.london.museum/support-us/

Foundations

Friends receive regular newsletters (now in digital form) with details of significant new acquisitions, information about particular aspects of the collections and occasional book reviews. Exclusive events for Friends include talks and private views of exhibitions.

Contributions from Friends assist in the development of the Library & Museum, help to fund acquisitions and support the conservation of the collections.

William Preston and the Prestonian Lecture

The Prestonian Lecture is the only official lecture held under the authority of the United Grand Lodge of England. The lecturer is appointed on the nomination of the Board of General Purposes by the Trustees of the Prestonian Fund and the lecture is given officially on at least four occasions, and at least twice in London. The lecture is also given unofficially during and after the Prestonian year both in Great Britain and overseas. Lodges who wish to host the lecture officially do so by contacting the Grand Secretary through Metropolitan, Provincial or District Grand Secretaries.

The Lectureship is a memorial to William Preston (1742-1818) an author, printer and the foremost Masonic educator of his age, who left a legacy to Grand Lodge for this purpose.

Lectures were given in Preston's name from 1820 until 1862, when the programme went into abeyance. The Prestonian Lectureship was revived in 1924 with the modification that the lecturer would give a talk on a subject of his own choosing. The Prestonian Lecture has been given annually since that date with the exception of the years 1940-46.

William Preston was born in Edinburgh on 28 July 1742 and educated at the Royal High School and the University of Edinburgh. He took employment as secretary to the classicist and grammarian Thomas Ruddiman (1654-1757) who, suffering from poor health, arranged for Preston to be apprenticed to his brother, Walter, a printer and publisher.

Armed with a letter of introduction from Walter Ruddiman, Preston moved to London in 1760 where he obtained work with William Strahan (1715-1785), later the King's Printer.[168]

---

[168] H.R. Tedder, 'Preston, William (1742–1818)', rev. Jeffrey Makala, *Oxford Dictionary of National Biography*, (Oxford: Oxford University Press, 2004).

Preston was employed initially as a 'principal corrector' and over time rose steadily through the ranks being promoted to superintendent and thereafter editor. In 1804, Strahan's son, Andrew, who had inherited the business from his father, made Preston a full partner in the firm.

Strahan's was during Preston's time with the firm one of the largest print houses in London and reputedly the most profitable. The company printed and published a broad range of popular and notable authors and as it expanded Preston benefited accordingly.

Preston's interest in freemasonry appears to have dated from the early 1760s when a group of Edinburgh men resident in London formed a Masonic lodge, number 111, under the auspices of the Antients Grand Lodge. The lodge was warranted in 1763 and met at the *White Hart* tavern in the Strand. A year later, the lodge took a new constitution under the auspices of the Moderns – the original Grand Lodge of England – and a new name: Caledonian Lodge.

The Moderns' warrant was granted on 15 November 1764 with the lodge receiving the number 325.[169] It met at the Half Moon Tavern on Cheapside in the City of London. The lodge still exists and is now numbered No. 134. It meets at Mark Masons' Hall – 86 St James's Street – in central London.[170]

Preston was reportedly the second man to be initiated into the lodge and was reputedly instrumental in the transfer of lodge jurisdiction from 'Antients' to 'Moderns'. On becoming Master of the lodge he undertook

To inform myself fully of the general rules of the Society, that I might be able to fulfil my own duty and officially enforce obedience in others.

Preston subsequently became Master of several other London lodges and simultaneously began his research into freemasonry and to develop a series of lectures to explain the different Masonic degrees. The success of his orations was such that he was

---

[169] Lane's *Masonic Records*.
[170] *Ibid.*

able to publish his lectures in 1772 as *Illustrations of Freemasonry*. The work ran to some seventeen editions and was complemented by a series of catechetical lectures explaining the three Craft degrees.

In 1774, Preston visited the Lodge of Antiquity, previously the Goose & Gridiron, one of the four lodges that had founded the first Grand Lodge of England. He was invited to become a joining member in June 1774 and possibly as a means of arresting a decline in membership numbers had within two weeks been invited to become Master.

The lodge flourished during Preston's three and a half years in the Chair and Preston's status was acknowledged by his being appointed Deputy Grand Secretary as well as 'Printer to the Society'.[171]

The reputation of the Lodge of Antiquity was later enhanced by the Duke of Sussex, subsequently the first Grand Master of the United Grand Lodge of England, who became a member and Master of the lodge.

---

[171] Gordon Hills, *Brother William Preston, an Illustration of the Man, his Methods and his Work*. Prestonian Lecture, 1927.

In December 1777, partly as a result of personal disputes within the lodge, Preston and others members of the Lodge of Antiquity were reported to Grand Lodge for apparently disregarding Grand Lodge's standing orders by appearing in public in their Masonic regalia. They were accused of taking part in a Masonic procession albeit that they were simply returning to the lodge from a nearby church service. A formal complaint against them was investigated and Preston was expelled after he claimed that the Lodge of Antiquity, as a 'Time Immemorial' lodge, pre-dated the Grand Lodge and was thus not subject to the rules of Grand Lodge.

Preston subsequently led a breakaway group from the Lodge of Antiquity and an authority was sought and subsequently obtained from a rival grand lodge – the Grand Lodge of York – to establish 'the Grand Lodge of England South of the River Trent', of which Preston later became Deputy Grand Master.

The dispute was resolved a decade later in May 1789 with Preston's apology. Honour satisfied, Preston was welcomed back to the Grand Lodge of England and in 1790 the Lodge of Antiquity was re-united. The Grand Lodge of England South of the River Trent had ceased to exist the prior year.

William Preston died on 1 April 1818 at his home at Dean Street in central London and was buried on 10 April in St Paul's Churchyard by St Paul's Cathedral. Under the terms of his Will he bequeathed an endowment of £300 to Grand Lodge to provide for the annual delivery of a lecture, the lecturer to be appointed by the Grand Master.

The Prestonian Lecturer is appointed each year and charged with delivering a lecture on a Masonic subject of his choosing to 'instruct and entertain a general Lodge audience'.

About the Author

The Prestonian Lecturer for 2016, Dr Richard (Ric) Berman, is an authority on eighteenth-century English, Irish and American freemasonry. He has published six books that examine different aspects of the Craft in its formative years: Each looks at freemasonry within a mainstream historical perspective and reveals how the Craft evolved as it reflected and interacted with contemporary society.

The Foundations of Modern Freemasonry (now in its second edition) has been described as a 'walk through Hanoverian England and its players' that offers 'a critical and crucial insight into the Fraternity's underpinnings that helps set the historical record straight'.

'The transformation of English Freemasonry after the foundation of the Grand Lodge of England in 1717 was especially marked by the (largely nominal) leadership of young pro-Hanoverian Whig aristocrats who transformed Freemasonry into an important component of the economic, scientific, social, and political changes of the eighteenth century. Freemasonry rapidly became an important facet of the upper reaches of English society, and Berman (Oxford) traces the role these aristocratic architects played in the formation of what quickly became the most prominent and socially elite fraternal order of the modern era. There were important connections between Freemasonry and the judiciary, the Royal Society, and other learned and professional societies. Berman provides a useful introduction to these key figures, as well as a series of valuable appendixes, giving readers the Grand Officers of the Grand Lodge of England, excerpts from the Masonic 1723 Constitutions, a list of the various military lodges, and an inventory of the Masonic membership of selected professional societies... a valuable work for serious Masonic historians. Recommended.' --*Choice*

Schism takes the Masonic story further, exploring the creation of the Antients Grand Lodge and Antients Freemasonry, and tracing the influence of Ireland and the London Irish, and especially Laurence Dermott, the Antients' Grand Secretary. The work reveals the social accessibility of Antients Freemasonry and contrasts this with the relative exclusivity of the 'Moderns' and the original Grand Lodge of England.

The growing antipathy between the Moderns and Antients instigated what became a six decades-long rivalry. The dispute led to alterations being made to the Moderns' ritual to accommodate the more traditional approach of the Antients, and to changes to the composition of freemasonry's membership, extending Masonic sociability more broadly.

Schism offers one of the most detailed studies of the subject and supplements and replaces outdated Masonic histories. The book has been praised as adding to the understanding of English and Irish history in the eighteenth century and especially that of the lower middling and London Irish and their social and trade networks. It offers a Masonic prism through which Britain's calamitous relationship with Ireland can be examined.

'Understanding the past and the conditions that existed during the formation of Freemasonry provides a lens by which to view the Craft and understand its relationship with the world today. *Schism: The Battle that Forged Freemasonry* provides such a lens and is an excellent addition to Berman's *The Foundations of Modern Freemasonry*.' - John R. Bo Cline, *The Journal of The Masonic Society,* 2014.

Foundations and *Schism* have been praised as 'the most important books on English Freemasonry published in recent times' and 'rethinking the relationship between Moderns and Antients'.

*L*oyalists *&* Malcontents provides a unique perspective to the interplay between Britain and its North American colonies. The book exposes the social and political fissures that caused American society and American Freemasonry to fracture in the late eighteenth century. It details for the first time how freemasonry emerged in South Carolina and Georgia in the 1730s, and traces its evolution through to the War of Independence and its aftermath.

The wealth generated by the plantation system in South Carolina and Georgia underpinned Southern Society and was supportive of Southern Freemasonry to the extent that the introduction of slavery into Georgia transformed the Lodge at Savannah from a modest 'tippling society' into a facsimile of South Carolina's more affluent elite lodges.

Published in 2017, *Espionage, Diplomacy & the Lodge* unveils one of the early eighteenth century's most influential figures: Charles Delafaye, under-secretary of state, spy-master, magistrate and freemason. A member of the Horn Tavern lodge, Delafaye was at the centre of Whitehall's inner circle and a conduit for intelligence from the Secret Department of the Post Office and its Deciphering Branch. Loyal and efficient, he orchestrated the government's anti-Jacobite endeavours for two decades. The books provides a glimpse into Britain's early secret services and explains the cross-over between freemasonry, espionage and diplomacy.

Before beginning a second career as an academic, lecturer and author, Dr Berman worked in investment management, latterly as chief executive of an institutional fund manager. He holds a Masters in Economics from the University of Cambridge and a Doctorate in History from the University of Exeter; he is a Visiting Research Fellow at Oxford Brookes University, a Fellow of the Royal Historical Society and a Life Fellow of the Huguenot Society.

A freemason for forty years, Ric Berman is a Past Master of the Marquis of Dalhousie Lodge, No. 1159 (EC); Treasurer of Quatuor Coronati Lodge, No. 2076 (EC), England's oldest research lodge; and a Past Master of the Temple of Athene Lodge, No. 9541 (EC), the research lodge for the Province of Middlesex. He holds London and Provincial Grand Rank.

The Prestonian Lectures and Lecturers, 1924-2017

1924
The First Degree   C.W. Firebrace

1925
The Development of the
Trigradal System   L. Vibert

1926
The Evolution of the
Second Degree   L. Vibert

1927
Bro William Preston: the
Man, his Methods & Work   G.P.G. Hills

1928
Masonic Teachers of the
Eighteenth Century   J. Stokes

1929
The Antiquity of Our
Masonic Legends   R.H. Baxter

1930
The Seven Liberal Arts
and Sciences   H.D.C. de Lafontaine

1931
Medieval Master Masons
and their Secrets   W.W. Covey Crump

1932
The Evolution of
Masonic Ritual
in England in the
Eighteenth Century   J.H. Lepper

1933
The Old Charges in
Eighteenth Century Masonry H. Poole

1934
The Art, Craft, Science, or
'Mystery' of Masonry — F.C.C.M. Fighiera

1935
Freemasonry and
Contemplative Art — W.J. Bunney

1936
Freemasonry, Ritual
and Ceremonial — L. Edwards

1937
Inwardness of Masonic
Symbolism in the Three
Degrees — J. Johnson

1938
The Mason Word — D. Knoop

1939
Veiled in Allegory and
Illustrated by Symbols — G.E.W. Bridge

1940-1946 — *Lectures Suspended*

1947
The Grand Lodge South
of the River Trent   G.Y. Johnson

1948
The Deluge   F.L. Pick

1949
Our Oldest Lodge   C.C. Adams

1950
Lodges of Instruction, their
Origin and Development   W.I. Grantham

1951
Variations in Masonic
Ceremonial   H.W. Chetwin

1952
Free in Freemason:
The Idea of Freedom
through Six Centuries   B.E. Jones

1953
What is Freemasonry?   G.S. Shepherd-Jones

1954
The Freemason's Education — B.W. Oliver

1955
The Fellowship of Knowledge — J.R. Rylands

1956
The Making of a Mason — G.S. Draffen

1957
The Transition from Operative to Speculative Masonry — H. Carr

1958
The Years of Development — N. Rogers

1959
Medieval Organisation of Freemasons' Lodges — J.S. Purvis

1960
Growth of Freemasonry in England & Wales since 1717 — S. Pope

1961
King Solomon in the
Middle Ages									G. Brett

1962
The Grand Mastership
of HRH the Duke
of Sussex									P.R. James

1963
Folklore into Masonry					H.G.M. Clarke

1964
The Genesis of
Freemasonry								A.J. Arkell

1965
Brethren who Made
Masonic History							E. Newton

1966
The Evolution of the
English Provincial
Grand Lodge								W.R.S. Bathurst

1967
The Grand Lodge of England:
the First Hundred Years   A.R. Hewitt

1968
The Five Noble Orders
of Architecture   H.K. Atkins

1969
External Influences on
the Evolution of English
Masonry   J.R. Clarke

1970
In the Beginning
was the Word   E. Ward

1971
Masters and Master Masons   R. Tydeman

1972
'It is not in the power of
any man': a Study in Change   T.O. Haunch

1973
In Search of Ritual Uniformity   C.F.W. Dyer

1974
Drama and Craft   N. Barker Cryer

1975
Anthony Sayer, Gentleman:
the Truth at Last   T. Beck

1976
Preston's England   A.C.F. Jackson

1977
The Tyler or Outer Guard   R.A. Wells

1978
Grand Stewards 1728-1978   C. Mackechnie-Jarvis

1979
250 Years of Masonry
in India   G.E. Walker

1980
Robert Freke Gould   F.J. Cooper

1981
Grand Lodge of England
According to the
Old Institutions   C.N. Batham

1982
The Government
of the Craft   J. Stubbs

1983
The Pre-Eminence of the
Great Architect in
Freemasonry   R.H.S. Rottenbury

1984
Getting and Giving
Masonic Knowledge   H. Mendoza

1985
"not only Ancient but
useful and necessary":
Deacons   S. Bruce

1986
The Old Charges   W. McLeod

1987
The Role of the Innkeeper
in Masonry C. Gotch

1988
Music and Masonry A.I. Pearmain

1989
The Book of Constitutions
of UGLE Sir L. Brett

1990
The Master-Mason-at-Arms F. Smyth

1991
Freemasons at War K.T. Flynn

1992
Masonry: Pure and Applied M. Morgan

1993
"And the Greatest of
These is Charity" J.M. Hamill

1994
English Freemasonry
in Europe 1717-1919   M.L. Brodsky

1995
Freemasonry and Sport   J. Webb

1996
The Freemasons and the
Friendly Societies   J.F. Goodchild

1997
The Image of Freemasonry
in Popular Fiction   R.A. Gilbert

1998
Elias Ashmole:
the First Recorded
English Freemason   B.F. Page

1999
Freemasonry and
Entertainment   J.F. Ashby

2000
"for therein you will
be taught ..."   R.A. Crane

2001
The First Degree
in Freemasonry   S. Fernie

2002
The Anglo-Irish Masonic
Connections   C.W. Wallis-Newport

2003
The Contribution of
the Provinces to the
Development of English
Freemasonry   A.N. Newman

2004
English Freemasonry: Origins,
Themes & Developments   A.T. Stewart

2005
Women and Freemasonry   G.W.S. Davie

Ric Berman

2006
The Victoria Cross –
Freemasons' Band
of Brothers　　　　　　　　G.S. Angell

2007
Grand Secretaries of the
UGLE (1813-1980)　　　　R.B.F. Khambatta

2008
The Language of Ritual　　R. Sillett

2009
Go and Do Thou Likewise
(Masonic Processions)　　　J. Wade

2010
Music in Masonry
and Beyond　　　　　　　W. Warlow

2011
Was Sir Christopher
Wren a Freemason?　　　　J. Campbell

2012
Scouting and Freemasonry:
Two Parallel Organisations?　A.D.G. Harvey

2013
'As we were seen – the Press
and Freemasonry'　　　　　P.R. Calderwood

2014
1814 Consolidation and Change:
the first year of the United
Grand Lodge of England　　M.A. Kearsley

2015
Wherever Dispersed:
The Traveling Mason　　　R. Burt

2016
Foundations: new light
on the formation and
early years of the Grand
Lodge of England　　　　R.A. Berman

2017
The Grand Design　　　　J. Daniel

The Old
Stables
Press
• Oxfordshire •

www.ingramcontent.com/pod-product-compliance
Lightning Source LLC
Chambersburg PA
CBHW020003050426
42450CB00005B/294